Contents

Page

LIST OF ILLUSTRATIONS ii

INTRODUCTION 1

CLOSE AIR SUPPORT IN WORLD WAR II 6

CLOSE AIR SUPPORT IN THE KOREAN WAR 27

CLOSE AIR SUPPORT OPERATIONS AFTER THE KOREAN WAR 89

CONCLUSION 109

BIBLIOGRAPHY 113

Illustrations

Page

Figure 1. Army-Air Force Control System Southwest Pacific 1944 16

Figure 2. Navy-Marine Control System Southwest Pacific 1944 18

Figure 3. Joint Policy Agreement for Control of Aircraft Operating over Korea............49

Figure 4. Navy-Marine Control System Close Air Support Architecture during Amphibious operations Korea 51

Figure 5. Army-Air Force Control System Close Air Support Architecture during operations in Korea 53

Figure 6. Navy-Marine Request Procedures Korea 54

Figure 7. Navy-Marine Execution Procedures Korea 55

Figure 8. Army-Air Force Request Procedures Korea 56

Figure 9. Army-Air Force Execution Procedures Korea 57

Figure 10. Air Ground System US & Vietnamese 1968 97

Figure 11. Navy-Marine (III MAF) Air-Ground Control System 99

Chapter 1

INTRODUCTION

It is fully realized that the only excuse for aviation in any service is its usefulness in assisting the troops on the ground to successfully carry out their operations.

Major Alfred A. Cunningham, Marine Aviator number 1
"Value of Aviation to the Marine Corps", Marine Corps Gazette September 1920.

Marine aviation has one mission...that is to support the ground elements of the FMF.

Major General Keith B. McCutcheon, April 1969

Statement of the Research Question

The quotations above give some indication of the depth of commitment of the U.S. Marine Corps for aviation in the close air support mission. In the following chapters, I will examine that portion of Marine Corps history concerning the development of close air support (CAS) doctrine. The purpose of this study is to examine the historical record in terms of the development of Marine philosophy regarding CAS, and the conflict that arose among the armed services over the effective employment of CAS during the Korean War. I will also examine the development and impact of the single air manager, or Joint Force Air Component Commander (JFACC), on CAS employment. The controversy arose from the purported effectiveness of Marine CAS versus the alleged ineffective support provided by the U.S. Air Force. With Korea as a backdrop, I will examine and explain the Marine perspective on CAS and the distinction between the Marines and the Navy, the Air Force, and the Army in that regard.

In general, I will focus on the Marines' application of CAS from World War II to the Vietnam War; however, my emphasis will be on CAS during the Korean War. The examination of World War II will focus mainly on the Southwest Pacific Theater rather than the war in Europe. The intent is not to diminish the lessons of the war in Europe, but rather to focus on the Marine experience, which took place in the Pacific theater. By looking at World War II, I will establish the context for the doctrinal development of CAS as applied later in Korea. Then I will examine CAS in Vietnam. I will examine the extent to which the services reached a doctrinal solution concerning CAS and the single air asset manager.

The Korean War shaped the persistent argument concerning CAS employment among Marines, sailors, airmen, and soldiers regarding its value to a winning strategy. This study will explore the impact that General Keith B. McCutcheon, United States Marine Corps, had on CAS employment during the Korean War and how he influenced the CAS argument overall. I will discuss the evolution of General McCutcheon's views on CAS from World War II through the Vietnam War. The emphasis on his views across three decades provides a Marine practitioner's perspective regarding the CAS mission. My intent is to contrast McCutcheon's views on the most effective use of CAS with those views generally held by the Air Force, Navy, and Army.

General McCutcheon is the father of the Marine helicopter aviation. He was a helicopter squadron commander during the Korean War. He was also an attack and transport pilot during World War II and the years leading up to the Korean War influenced his ideas, opinions, and writings on CAS. General McCutcheon is one Marine who, through his writing and speaking, had an impact on CAS. He was not the only Marine voice on CAS during this period, but his life and writings provide a good case for understanding the Marine Corps argument for CAS as a method of employment. How did General McCutcheon come to his understanding of CAS? How did he arrive at the conclusion that CAS was a failure in the Korean War? How did he influence the debate concerning CAS employment and a single air manager? What were the lessons learned concerning CAS and the single air manager during the Korean War, and do they have value today? These are a few of the questions that, when answered, will provide an insight and understanding of Marine CAS.

Problem Background and Significance

The Korean War significantly shaped the views of each armed service concerning CAS employment and the future role and development of the JFACC. The CAS controversy during the Korean War resulted largely from the differing views regarding effectiveness among the armed services. The questions raised, seemingly every time we go to war, seem the same today as they were during the Korean War.

Limitations of the Study

The amount of work already done on the subject of the Korean War and CAS is considerable. I cannot hope to address all the issues associated with this subject. One of my colleagues, Michael Lewis, has already addressed the issue of CAS and the single air asset manager in Korea from an Army perspective. He used Lieutenant General Ned Almond as a subject in his 1996 School of Advanced Airpower Studies (SAAS) thesis, "Lieutenant General Ned Almond, USA: A Ground Commander's Conflicting View with Airmen over CAS Doctrine and Employment." General McCutcheon is not as outspoken and controversial as Lt. Gen. Almond. However, his personal papers provide the information necessary to identify the Marine philosophy of the period. My intent is to complement Lewis's study of CAS and command and control issues during the Korean War by using a comparable format, but focusing on the Marine perspective.

Lewis limited his study of CAS to four issues where the Air Force and Army had differing philosophies. I will use a similar framework to address how the Marine philosophy differed from that of the other services. The issues are: 1) airpower employment priorities; 2) the organization of CAS assets; 3) the means and effectiveness of command and control (C2); and 4) the aircraft basing debate. I will consider other contextual factors that may affect the evaluation of the Marine method of employing CAS. I will consider doctrine, tactics, techniques, and procedures; organization and employment of CAS systems and architecture; friendly capabilities, equipment, personnel, and training; threat and terrain; the CAS philosophy as it fits strategy; inter-service politics; and the historical tradition.

Definitions and Assumptions

I think it is important to identify a generally accepted definition of CAS. During World War II, the Korean War, and later in the Vietnam War, CAS was referred to by many names and meanings. CAS received various titles such as the close support of ground troops, tactical support, tactical air support, close support, and even co-operation.

The meaning of each varied with the number of tactical air tasks associated with the close support mission. FM 31-35 added to the confusion by prioritizing the associated tasks of close tactical support.[1] The General Headquarters, Southwest Pacific Area, defined Close Support in its Standard Operating Procedures (SOP) as "the employment of Air Force units for a specific purpose intimately associated with a definite operation of supported forces. Close support represents a definite and fixed obligation by the Air Force in connection with such an operation."[2] Sometimes the term close air support referred to the closeness of targets to friendly troops on the ground, while at other times it referred to the closeness of command, communication, and cooperation in the Army's zone of action.[3] These different definitions highlighted the lack of an approved joint doctrine and limited the flexibility of airpower in the CAS role.

General McCutcheon defined CAS as the use of aircraft as a close support weapon at the hands of the infantry commander, used against enemy forces and installations holding up the advance of his own forces. McCutcheon added that two critical elements were required to complete the definition of close air support. First, an appropriate means of control and communication was necessary to bring aviation fires sufficiently close to friendly troops to achieve the desired effect. Second, CAS may be employed in two ways, either against targets that cannot be reached by the commander's other weapons or in conjunction with the ground weapons in a coordinated attack.[4] A

---

[1] *Korean Evaluation Report on Air Operations* (Sterns Mission), Department of the Air Force, Washington, DC 16 Jan 1951, K168.041-2 USAF Historical Archives ASI (ASHAF) Maxwell AFB, AL 25 Jun – Dec 1950,v.1, 34.

[2] General Headquarters Southwest Pacific, Standing Operating Procedure (SOP) for CLOSE AIR SUPPORT instruction number 6, General MacArthur, Commanding, 24 June 1943, 1-2. (cover letter, Endorsing Memorandum, number 23:General Headquarters XIV Corps, Major General Griswald, Commanding, 10 Oct 1944. (Keith B. McCutcheon Personal Collection (PC) #464, Box 3, created by Regina Timmons, Marine Corps University Archives (MCUA), Quantico, VA, June 1996.)

[3] Dr. James A. Huston, "Tactical Use of Airpower: The Army Experience," *Military Review*, Command and General Staff College, Fort Leavenworth, KS, 32 no. 4 (July 1952), 37.

[4] Lieutenant Colonel Keith B. McCutcheon, "Close Air Support SOP," *Marine Corps Gazette* (Aug. 1945 29, no.8), 48. (Lieutenant Colonel McCutcheon wrote a draft paper entitled "Close Support Aviation," which was later edited into three articles and published by the *Marine Corps Gazette* under the following titles. "Close Air Support SOP," (Aug. 1945), 48-50; "Close Air Support on Luzon," (Sep 45, 29 no. 9), 38-39; and

more modern definition and the definition I adhere to in this study, of CAS is the use of air weapon systems in attack against hostile targets which are in close proximity to friendly forces and which require the detailed coordination and integration of each air mission with the fire and movement of friendly forces.

Preview of the Argument

I determined early in my research that the best approach to helping a reader understand the complex issues of Command and Control (C_2) and CAS development from World War II through the Vietnam War was to follow a framework similar to that of the Lewis paper I mentioned earlier. That is what I have done. The first task is to examine each of the CAS issues and the contextual factors affecting the three wars in which General McCutcheon participated. Second, I investigate CAS during WWII using the Philippines as a key case study. Third, I investigate CAS and C_2 applied during the Korea War. Fourth, I investigate CAS and C_2 during the Vietnam War and examine in particular General McCutcheon's view. Finally, I draw a few conclusions concerning CAS during this three-war period by readdressing the CAS issues and determine their relevance for today and into the future.

"Air Support Techniques," (Apr 46, 30 no. 4), 23-24 (K.B. McCutcheon, PC#464, Box 3, MCUA).

Chapter 2

CLOSE AIR SUPPORT IN WORLD WAR II

Close air support means that those bombs are so close that if you don't get in a hole or down as flat on your belly as you can, you're mighty likely to get your backside full of arrows.

Attributed to an unknown soldier on Mindanao,
WWII, by General C. Jerome.

Introduction: Setting the Stage

The notion to employ airplanes as flying artillery probably germinated soon after the airplane first took flight. By 1914 the US Army Field Regulation addressed the issue of using combined arms operations that integrated aviation with the other weapons of the day.[5]

> The development of the Marine system of tactical air support started at the Yser river in France, in October 1918, when a Marine pilot flying one-hundred miles per hour in his DeHavilland (DH-4) aircraft tossed twenty-five pound bombs out of the cockpit on the German trenches. [They did this] at the request of the infantry commanders and delivered this ordnance onto the enemy at a distance of about four hundred feet in front of the requesting infantry.[6]

A post World War I review board was convened in 1919 to consolidate lessons learned from each branch of the American Expeditionary Forces. The board report,

---

[5] Robert Frank Futrell, *Ideas, Concepts, Doctrine: Basic Thinking in the United States Air Force 1907-1960*, vol. 1 (Maxwell, AFB, AL: Air University Press, 1989), 17. (War Department, Office of the Chief of Staff, Field Service Regulations, United States Army, 1914, corrected to 31 July 1918 (Washington, D.C: Government Printing Office, 1918), 13, 20-21, 74).

[6] Major E.E. Bagnall, *et al.*, *FAC [Forward Air Controller] Course book*, Headquarters, Marine Air Control Group 2, 1st Marine Aircraft Wing, Fleet Marine Force, 26 August 1952, 1. Also see Alan R. Millett, *Semper Fidelis: The History of the United States Marine Corps* (Ontario: The Free Press, 1991), 310, and Major Alfred A. Cunningham, "Value of Aviation to the Marine Corps," *Marine Corps Gazette*, (September 1920), 225-26.

issued by Major General Joseph T. Dickman, President of the Commission, noted that the Air Service had developed four missions: observation, distance reconnaissance and bombing, aerial combat, and combat against ground troops. The Dickman Board's review of aerial combat against ground troops concluded that air support of ground troops was not well developed, but declared that air support held great potential as an effective and decisive weapon on the battlefield.[7] Interest in CAS grew after World War I; however, the Army Air Corps concentrated primarily on independent operations focusing on distance reconnaissance and bombing. The Marine Corps took as its primary interest the practical application of air support of troops in combat.

During the so-called small wars period of the 1920s and 1930s, the Marines organized air support for ground troops. Close air support in Nicaragua (1927-1933) gave the Marines a decided advantage in that campaign. Marine aviation began to develop an air doctrine that would complement later amphibious doctrine. Major Ross E. Rowell's small squadron grew from an obsolete force of DeHavilland scout bombers in 1927 to a composite squadron of Ford and Fokker transports, modern scout bombers, and amphibian aircraft, supporting Marine Brigade operations in 1933.[8] The Marines relied on a simple and reliable visual air-ground communication system, which communicated vital information from ground units to pilots flying overhead. The pilot saw the visual signal and flew on to a message line pickup point. He would hook the request from a line strung between two poles and having read it would fly on to directly support the ground commander's mission objective.[9] Sometimes the visual signal was a panel marker on the ground. The meaning was briefed to the pilots before their mission takeoff to coordinate the support necessary for breaking up ambushes, sieges, and other close support tasks.[10] The command and control of these aircraft, although rudimentary, was sufficient and effective because of the pilot's ability to fly low and slow over an area, which allowed him to identify friendly and hostile forces.[11]

---

[7] Futrell, *Ideas, Concepts, Doctrine*, 28.
[8] Millett, 244, 249, and 252.
[9] MajGen V. E. McGee, "Tactical Air Support for Ground Forces," *Marine Corps Gazette* (December 1955), 13.
[10] Ibid.
[11] Ibid.

The issues and experiences of early combat aviation in World War I and the interwar years leading up to World War II contributed to the development of aviation doctrine that each of the services would pursue into World War II. The Nicaraguan experience gave the Marines a grasp of what CAS could provide a ground force. These combat experiences helped to solidify dive–bombing techniques and tactics, which Marine Lieutenant L.H.M. Sanderson had introduced and first attempted in 1919.[12] These techniques proved very effective and helped persuade Marine pilots and infantrymen alike that the purpose of aviation was to support surface operations.

In the 1930s, Marines tied aviation to amphibious landings because of necessity. Aviation in landing operations found a natural niche, filling the gap created by the flat-trajectory and high-velocity rounds often fired by naval weapons in the 1930s. Moreover, there was little money or ammunition to train naval gunners in shore bombardment and the sustained firing required in training destroyed the gun liners' rifling. This shortfall of capability was exacerbated by budget demands that focused Navy resources and facilities on building capital ships, and little Navy money was diverted to building amphibious transports or training for assault landings. The issue of air support for assault landings was further complicated by advancements in aircraft capabilities in terms of speed and firepower as compared to slower advancements in communication technology.

To get around this problem of funding capabilities, and training limitations, Marine aviation tied itself to two missions that would affect the initial development of attack aviation in a close support role during World War II, and ensure the future survival of Marine fixed wing aviation until the present. Marine leaders, such as Major Roy Geiger and Major Ross E. Rowell trained Marine aviators for landing force operations, but in order to receive top-of-the line planes the Marines took on the secondary missions of the defending advanced naval bases as well as the replacement squadrons for carrier-based aircraft.[13]

---

[12] Wray Johnson, "Biplanes and Bandits: The Early U.S. Airpower Experience in Small Wars," (Draft Paper, School of Advanced Airpower Studies (SAAS), 2001), 18. Also see Millett, *Semper Fidelis,* 333.

[13] Millett, Semper Fidelis.329-35.

World War I and the interwar years provided the backdrop to the Marine Corps' tactical air concepts for CAS that it took into World War II. Budget, organization, and mission issues affected the training, equipment, and employment capabilities of airpower in a CAS role. Indeed, these issues had a negative impact on cooperation among the armed services at the beginning of World War II. As that conflict progressed and air support missions became more important, CAS matured, the war had a dramatic impact on the close support in terms of creating an operational and/or strategic effects.

Still, important issues remained: 1) airpower employment priorities; 2) the organization of CAS assets; 3) the means and effectiveness of command and control (C2); and 4) the aircraft basing debate for CAS. The previous section illustrated some of the contextual factors that affected the evolution of Marine CAS employment. The preceding section also briefly outlined the doctrine, techniques, tactics, and procedures as well as the organization and employment of the CAS that gave Marine aviation a philosophy that complemented its amphibious warfare doctrinal development, thus creating a tradition, which informs Marine air support concepts today.

World War II and CAS Doctrine

The priority of CAS rises and falls in relation to other aviation missions and as the character of the war changes. In times of peace, CAS is generally a forgotten air mission. During times of war, the value and necessity for CAS may rise with a determined and combative enemy. The requirement for successful ground operations may include CAS as a priority and in turn influence the campaign plan and strategy of the theater Commander-in-Chief. CAS requires training preparation, coordination, and integration of the many commands and assets that are necessary to perform the mission. CAS is part of what John Sbrega calls a "tactical trinity," that is, the mission of air superiority, interdiction, and CAS.[14]

The strategic, operational, and tactical situation determines the mission priority among CAS, interdiction, and air superiority. As the situation changes so too would the mission priority. These tactical missions at times are subordinate to strategic attack, and

---

[14] John Sbrega, "Southeast Asia," in *Case Studies in the Development of Close Air Support*, ed. Benjamin Franklin Cooling, (Washington, DC: OAFH, 1990), 413.

vice versa. No single mission type can dominate training, planning, and execution at the expense of the other. The tug of war within and among the services over the proper use of aviation only adds to a generally poor initial showing of aviation in coordinating the efforts of air and ground units.[15]

The two theaters of war in World War II produced two very different and distinctive approaches to applying airpower. Separated along service lines and based on airpower employment priorities, two distinctive systems of command and control of air assets also developed during World War II, a Navy and Marine system of CAS, and an Air Force and Army system. The Navy and Marine system was tied to amphibious doctrine, established years earlier but not practiced to the level of proficiency necessary for immediate and successful execution. The Army and Air Force system relied on initiative in the combat zone to make up for the limited attention that CAS had received as a topic during the inter-war years.[16] However, doctrine was established over time in the form of unit standing operating procedures (SOP) and Field Manuals, such as FM 1–5 (1940), FM 31–35 (1942), and FM 100–20 (1943).

Airpower Employment Priorities

From the outset of the war, air missions were seemingly arranged in a fixed set of priorities. The prevailing operational understanding in all air forces was to secure air superiority as the most efficient and effective contribution to ground operations.[17] Nearly everyone agreed that achieving air superiority was the key to freedom of action on the surface and in the air. The next priority for air action was interdiction of lines of communication and isolation of the battlefield. Combined action with ground forces usually was third in terms of priority. Almost everyone agreed that these priorities were sound, but there was considerable divergence of opinion between the Army-Air Force

---

[15] McGee, 13.
[16] Joe Gray Taylor, "American Experience in the Southwest Pacific," in *Case Studies in the Development of Close Air Support*, ed. Benjamin Franklin Cooling, (Washington, DC: OAFH, 1990), 298.
[17] W. A. Jacobs, "The Battle for France, 1944," in *Case Studies in the Development of Close Air Support*, ed. Benjamin Franklin Cooling, (Washington, DC: OAFH, 1990), 251.

and the Navy-Marines regarding the value of CAS to the war effort and its impact in terms of creating strategic effect.

Timing was a critical question raised by the services about the integration of CAS into operations. The timing of CAS affected all levels of war. The shift in effort from isolation of the battlefield to CAS affects the operational/strategic situation. The Army and Air Force saw great benefit in apportioning a large number of sorties to interdiction and strategic attack, which would produce results similar to CAS over a longer time by choking off equipment, supplies, and reinforcements and at less risk to aircrews.

The Navy and Marines considered direct air support of ground units to be crucial for successful landing operations. Shifting the air effort away from close support potentially had a critical impact on the ground commander and his unit's effectiveness. The responsiveness of air assets to the ground commander's request seemingly had an impact on the perceived effectiveness of CAS during World War II. The battle for Tarawa illustrates the impact of CAS not being timely when the bombers detailed for the assault phase were twenty-five minutes late over their assigned targets, which caused the pre-assault bombardment to begin to early. The result was a shocking number of casualties at Tarawa, which prompted General Holland Smith to ask for a Marine Air Wing to fly in direct support of landing operations from fast carriers.[18]

The landing on Saipan was plagued by long delays between the issuing of a request for air support from the regiment or battalion in contact with the enemy until the aircraft reported on station and dropped their ordnance. The lag at Saipan between request and execution averaged an hour or more. The mission delay resulted from the poor communication architecture and control, centralized at the command level. The approval processes required the commander to positively clear a request before launching an aircraft.[19] The ground units also unflanked by the decision to redirect the air effort away from Saipan to the Battle of the Philippine Sea, when supporting carrier aviation had to leave Saipan to fight a naval engagement.[20]

---

[18] Jeter A. Isely and Philip A. Crowl, *The Marines and Amphibious War: Its Theory, and Its Practice in the Pacific* (Princeton, N.J.: Princeton University Press, 1951), 231.
[19] Ibid., 334.
[20] Futrell, 175.

These examples reinforced the idea prominent among Marines that "CAS was an additional weapon at the hands of the ground commander to be used against enemy forces and installations holding up the advance of his own lines."[21] As noted above, CAS was a necessary weapon in landing operations and supported the mission of the Fleet Marine Force in amphibious landings. The landing force commander could use CAS effectively to attack targets that his other weapons could not reach, and in conjunction with ground weapons in a coordinated attack.[22]

The Marine Corps amphibious assault mission required a natural reliance on CAS to support landing operations and amphibious targets that naval gunfire and the Marines limited organic artillery could not range. The Armies traditional land warfare role structured its fire support around armies, divisions, and corps heavily equipped with artillery. The Marines found it difficult to move heavy guns and ammo ashore in the volume necessary to support combat action during an assault. CAS provided the necessary fire support needed in the amphibious objective area to answer this tooth to tail dilemma. Therefore, the Marines relied more heavily on CAS as a substitute for artillery. Where it was possible, Marines used artillery and Naval gunfire to provide a cheaper means to put explosives on target rather than aircraft.

In the early days of the Luzon Campaign Lieutenant Colonel Russell Volckmann's guerrillas operated outside the range of artillery, Naval gunfire, and without tanks relying only on their rifles, automatic weapons, and a few mortars.[23] CAS was coordinated and Marine dive bombers provided the necessary fire support for Volckmann's light force to gain success.

The Army and Air Force view was that air employed in the ground force zone of contact was usually difficult to control, expensive, the least effective use of air employment, and should be done only at a critical time during the ground action when

---

[21] Lieutenant Colonel Keith B. McCutcheon, USMC, "Close Air Support Aviation", Group Operations Officer,
Marine Aircraft Group-24, First Marine Aircraft Wing, Staff Notes Report on Training Problems post Philippines Campaign October 1944, MCUA, PC#464, box 3, 5 April 1967), 121.
[22] Ibid., 122.
[23] Holt McAloney, "Is Air Support Effective," The Marine Corps Gazette (November 1945), 38.

such missions would be most profitable.[24] The Army and Air Force seemed determined to force a decision through strategic bombing and counter-air operations. The result was to minimize close support and to put an end to control by ground commanders."[25]

A driving force behind the development of a formal doctrine was General George Marshall, the Army Chief of Staff. In April 1943 he directed the writing of FM 100–20, "*Command and Employment of Airpower.*"[26] Marshall recognized the need for a manual based principally upon British and American experiences in North Africa which described the relationship between air and ground commanders and the concepts of airpower. Field Marshal Sir Bernard Montgomery, quoted in *Time* Magazine on 14 August 1944 stated that he "believed that though a tactical air force must be integrated with the ground forces it must not be tied in piecemeal lots to the ground units. Its function must be massed, theater wide and deep penetrations to fill the gap between tactical and strategic operations."[27] What General Marshall had done was attempt to bring some order into a haphazard collection of ideas and concepts concerning the employment of airpower in support of ground troops, an area where there was little agreement beyond the basic priorities of tactical airpower.

"The Field Manual first published on 21 July 1943, established the doctrine, organization, command requirements, and strategy of a tactical air force".[28] The manual gave indications to some ground force leaders that this was a not-so-subtle move toward Air Force independence and control of operation. The following extract from FM 100–20 might easily lead one to agree with that interpretation:

> Land power and airpower are co–equal and, interdependent forces; neither is an auxiliary of the other.
>
> The gaining of air superiority is the first requirement for the success of any major land operation…land forces operating without air superiority must take extensive security measurers against hostile air attack that their mobility and ability to defeat the enemy land forces are greatly reduced. Therefore, air forces must be employed primarily against the enemy's air forces until air superiority is obtained.

---

[24] Jacobs, 251.
[25] Dr. James A. Huston, "The Tactical Use of Air Power during World War II: The Army Experience," *Military Review* (July 1952), 33.
[26] David Syrett, "The Tunisian Campaign, 1942-43," in *Case Studies in the Development of Close Air Support*, ed. Benjamin Franklin Cooling, (Washington, DC: OAFH, 1990), 184.
[27] McCutcheon, 128.
[28] Ibid., 184.

The inherent flexibility of airpower is its greatest asset. This flexibility makes it possible to employ the whole weight of the available airpower against selected areas in turn…control of available airpower must be centralized and command must be exercised through the air force commander…the superior commander will not attach army air forces under his command except when such ground force units are operating independently or are isolated by distance or lack of communication."[29]

The manual's main points voiced five key issues. First, it stressed the principle of co-equality between the ground and air commanders; no longer would the air force be subordinate to the ground force. Second, the passage implied that the Air Force could act on its own as an independent force. Third, FM 100-20 set priorities for the air effort. Fourth, command of tactical air assets was centralized at the theater commander level. And fifth, the requirement to maintain the flexibility of aviation to mass when required to attack decisive targets restricted the CAS mission to an exclusionary mission.[30] The problem with this doctrinal publication and others, aside from the disagreements on terms and concepts of control, was that no one seemed to follow it.[31]

In the Pacific, the SOP for CAS issued by Headquarters XIV Corps was stated in a covering endorsement memorandum to subordinate units on 10 October 1944. The cover document forwarded two SOPs on CAS from General Headquarters Southwest Pacific, General MacArthur, Commanding. The cover memorandum pointed out that SOP number 6, published in 1943, established procedures for CAS operations in support of normal land warfare and that SOP number 16/2, also published in 1944, established procedures for CAS in support of landing (amphibious) operations. The XIV Corps memorandum clearly states that the two SOPs, although similar in most respects, were in conflict due to limitations of aircraft type and differences between Navy and Army aircraft providing CAS.[32]

---

[29] Huston, 33; Field Manual (FM) 100-20, *Command an Employment of Air Power*, July 1943.
[30] Syrett, 185; Huston, 33.
[31] Taylor, 311.
[32] James T. Walsh, Colonel, Adjutant General, General Headquarters XIV Corps, Major General Griswald, Commanding, Staff Memorandum number 23, Subject: SOP for Close Air Support, 10 Oct 1944. Quantico, VA: MCUA, PC#464, Box 3.

See the diagram of the two systems for CAS: Figure 1, The Army-Air Force Control System Southwest Pacific 1944, and Figure 2, The Navy-Marine Control System Southwest Pacific 1944.

The history of operations in the theater reveals that SOPs were not followed to the letter of the instruction due to personnel and equipment limitations. The result was that the procedures used were a mix of methods adapted to the situation at the time. This action led to problems in coordinating CAS at the unit level. Units requesting CAS support were not familiar with the non-standard procedures and CAS was neither effective nor efficient. Units were not familiar with the techniques, tactics, capabilities of aircraft, or their weapons and munitions.[33]

---

[33] Ibid.

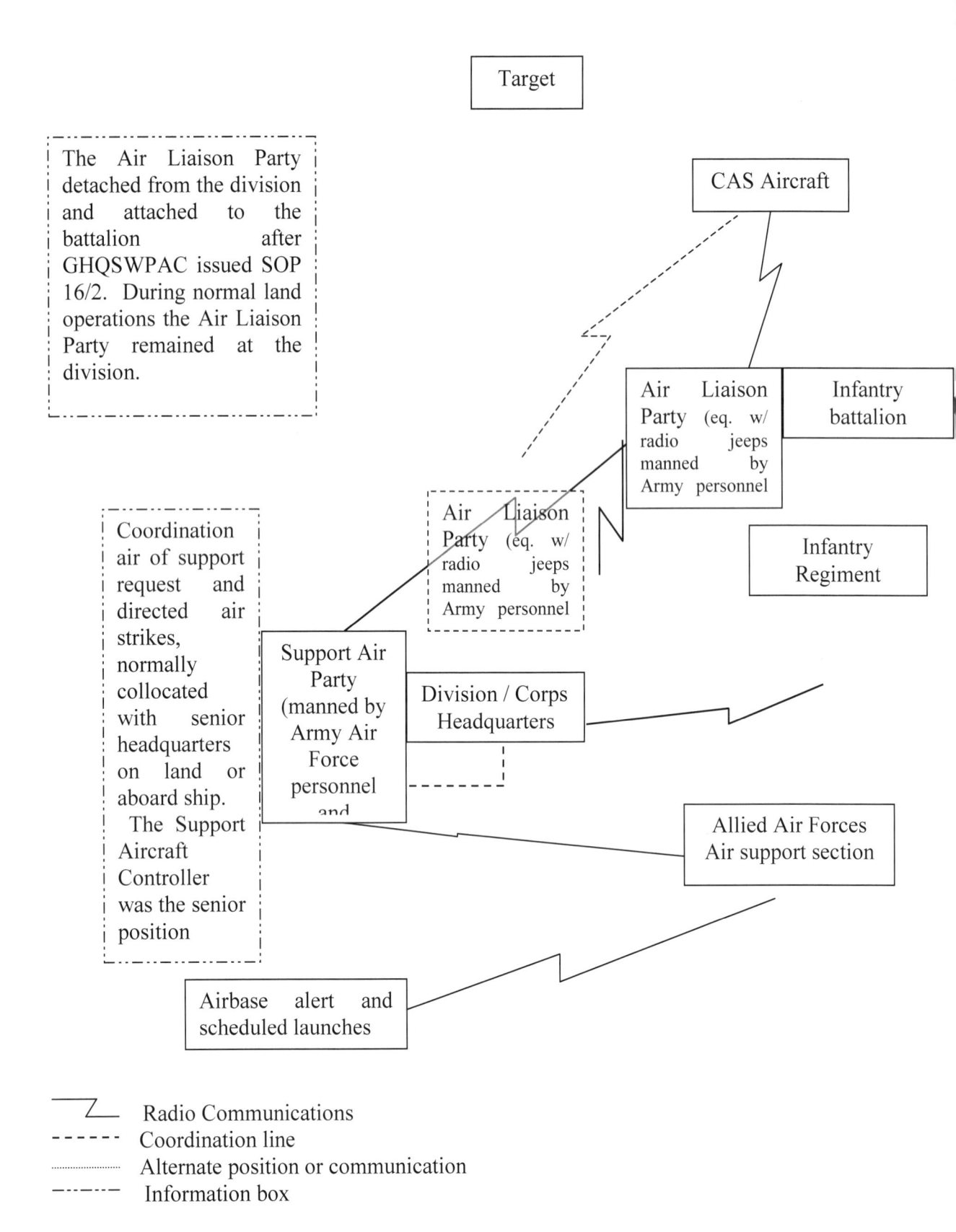

Figure 1. Army-Air Force Control System Southwest Pacific 1944

ALP	Battalion

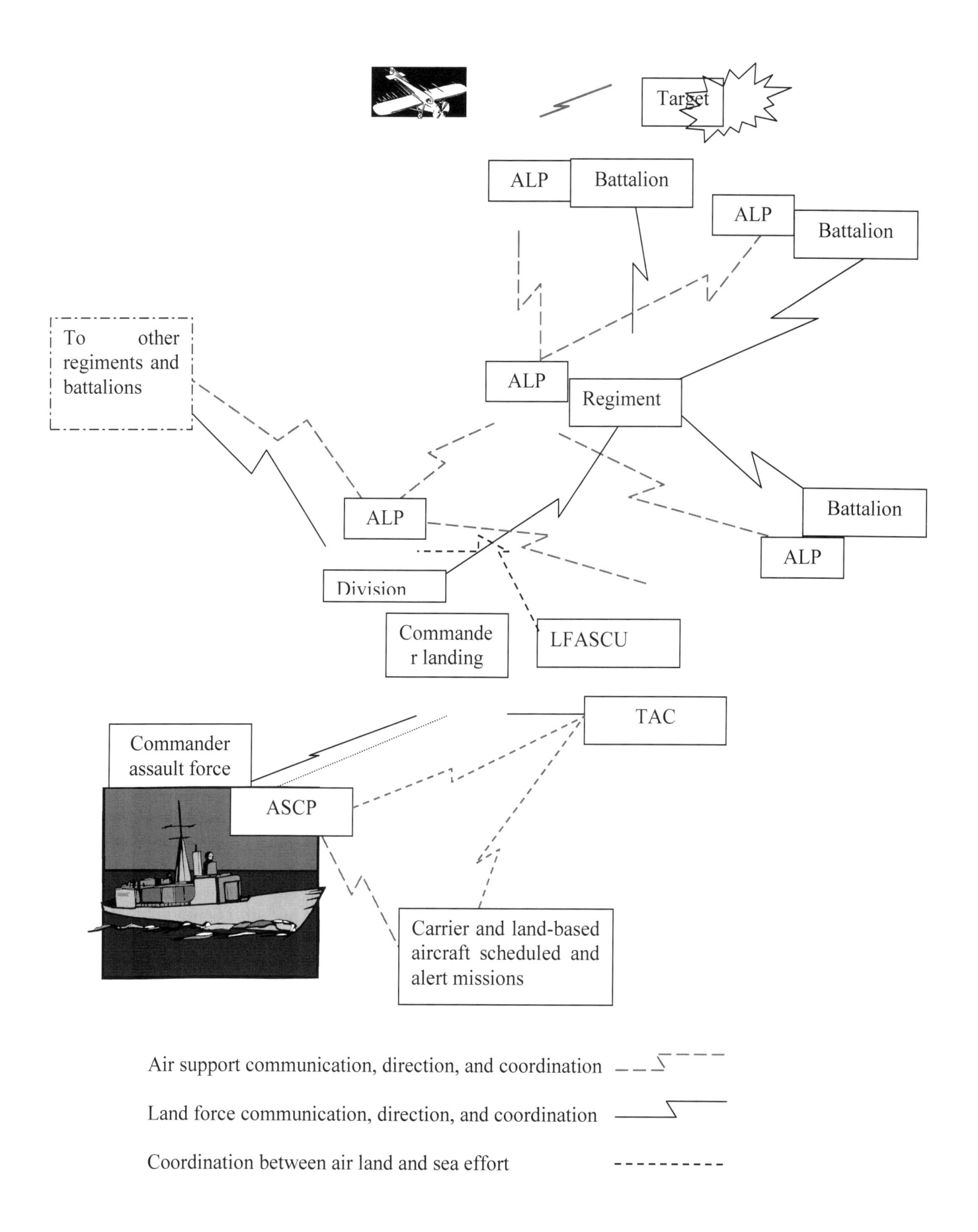

ALP	Battalion

To other regiments and battalions

ALP	Regiment

	Battalion
ALP	

ALP
Division

Commander landing	LFASCU

TAC

Commander assault force
ASCP

Carrier and land-based aircraft scheduled and alert missions

Air support communication, direction, and coordination ---⌐

Land force communication, direction, and coordination ——⌐

Coordination between air land and sea effort ----------

17

Figure 2. Navy-Marine Control System Southwest Pacific 1944

The points spelled out in FM 100–20 were gleaned from experiences learned primarily in Europe and North Africa, as well as the Far East Air Forces (FEAF) under the command of General George C. Kenney. Kenney's vision for the employment of his tactical air force prioritized the air missions similarly to what was later published in FM 100–20. He focused air assets first on gaining air superiority by defeating the enemy air forces, and then to isolating the battlefield by control of the sea lines of communication using air assets. Finally, when the battlefield was isolated, the air forces could be directed to support ground force operations. General Kenney rejected the establishment of Air Support Command in the Pacific Theater as directed by Washington and FM 31–35.[34] Air Support Command was to have sent airmen to act as advisors and to support ground commanders on air issues. Kenney rejected the advisors, sending them back, but kept their equipment and support personnel.[35]

Different theaters produced different systems based on very different terrain, weather, and fighting style. Large armies fighting long, drawn out campaigns across a continent characterized the European and North African theaters. The campaigns in the Southwest Pacific were amphibious, short, and very bloody, usually in small land areas. Surprisingly, the priorities for employment of CAS were not too different between the theaters. On the other hand, the doctrine, techniques, tactics, and procedures tended to shift in application and execution due in some measure to differences in organization.

The Organization of CAS Assets

Field Manual 31-35, and a year later FM 100-20, were published in an attempt to organize and employ air support systems and architecture that had gained some success in North Africa. They did fit well with the FEAF concepts of airpower after 1943.[36] The reality, however, was that from unit to unit, and operation-to-operation, through the whole length of World War II, the CAS command and control organization evolved with the change in the situation. Indeed, two systems emerged.[37] The Army-Air Force

---

[34] Taylor, 310-311.
[35] Ibid., 298.
[36] Ibid.
[37] MeGee, 13.

concept of air support became air co-operation, moving away from a unified command organization.[38] The Army-Air Force desired centralized, positive control of air assets organized under the Theater Air Commander. The Navy and the Marines developed a similar system but differed slightly in organization and function. The Navy and Marines practiced decentralized control of air support assets organized under a Tactical Air Commander subordinate to the Attack Force Commander.

Under the Army-Air Force system, air co-operation was necessary only at the numbered Air Force and Army level. The organization reflected the tactical air control system adopted in the European theater, which was an adaptation of the system employed in Italy. In the battles of France and Germany, the Ninth Air Force cooperated with the Twelfth Army Group, and Third Army received outstanding air support as it marched through France.[39]

In the Pacific, General MacArthur and his headquarters issued SOP Instruction number 6 in 1943, which directed and obligated Air Force units to support ground units' requests for air support. "Close Air Support represents a definite and fixed obligation by the Air Force in connection with operations."[40] The SOP went on to charge the Commander, Allied Air Forces, with providing CAS to the task forces. Additionally, the SOP charged the Commander, Allied Air Forces, with thorough planning of operations and an emphasis on teamwork and training in collaboration with other combat headquarters.[41]

The fundamental unit of the Army-Air Force organization was the Support Air Party (SAP). Normally located at the division or corps level, its purpose was to coordinate air support requests and direct air strikes. Two Air Force aviators and other support personnel manned each SAP. The SAP connected with the ALP via a jeep mounted radio communication set, the SRC-399. The ALPs were manned by Army

---

[38] Taylor, 311.
[39] Futrell, 174.
[40] General Headquarters, Southwest Pacific Area, Standing Operation Procedure instruction, no.6, Close Air Support, 24 June 1943, 2. (Noted hereafter as: GHQSPA SOP no.6)(Keith B. McCutcheon Personal Collection (PC) #464, Box 3, created by Regina Timmons, Marine Corps University Archives (MCUA), Quantico, VA, June 1996.)
[41] GHQSPA SOP no.6, 3.

personnel and were organic to the table of organization at the unit level of the division.[42]

In 1944, MacArthur's headquarters published SOP Instruction 16/2, *Cooperative Action Land–based and Carrier–based Aircraft Support of Landing Operations*, the intent of which was to encourage greater cooperation in landing operations and signified the acknowledgment of a difference in operational CAS requirements. The key organizational difference was the establishment of the Air Liaison Party (ALP). The ALP was attached to the Infantry battalion. SOP number 6 does not list this position and implied that the Support Air Controller (SAC) would be the lowest position manned by Air Force personnel at the division level or higher. SOP number 16/2 does not identify who was to man the ALP by service, experience, or job title. It simply states that this "small communications team would report the position of frontline troops, results of missions, and the location of remunerative targets" to the SAC, an air officer, aboard the headquarters ship, or with the SAP ashore on the landing beach. The SAC went ashore when the tactical situation permitted and assisted the SAC afloat (the senior position) with coordination of air support assets. The organizational result of this SOP appeared to move the Army air control closer to the Navy–Marine system when conducting landing operations.[43]

The Navy–Marine CAS organization placed the command of air support assets in the hands of the Amphibious Attack Force Commander during the initial stages of amphibious operations.[44] He exercised command through the Tactical Air Commander

---

[42] Lieutenant Colonel Keith B. McCutcheon, USMC, "Air Support Techniques," *Marine Corps Gazette* (April 1946), 23, 24. (McCutcheon papers MCUA, PC#464, box 3, contains a draft copy of this article titled: "Army Air Support System").

[43] General Headquarters, Southwest Pacific Area, Standing Operation Procedure instruction, no.16/2, Close Air Support, 26 September1944, 1, 2. (Noted hereafter as: GHQSPA SOP no.16/2)(Keith B. McCutcheon Personal Collection (PC) #464, Box 3, created by Regina Timmons, Marine Corps University Archives (MCUA), Quantico, VA, June 1996.); GHQSPA SOP no. 6, 3, 4.

[44] Headquarters Marine Corps, "An Evaluation of Air Operations Affecting the U.S. Marine Corps in World War II", 31 December 1945 (Washington, D.C.: HQMC 1945), II-10. (Keith B. McCutcheon Personal Collection (PC) #464, Box 4. This document includes cover letters dated 11 October 1945 Serial MC 558459 from CMC General Vandergrift to the senior member of the board to re-examine adequacy of present concept missions and functions of the Marine Corps. The senior member was General M.B. Twining, Commanding General, Marine Corps Schools)

(TAC) who was located aboard the flagship. The amphibious attack force commander transferred command and control functions to the commander of the landing force ashore in later phases of the amphibious operation. The TAC would then move to the command post ashore to exercise air operations.[45]

The control organization elements of the Navy–Marine system for CAS included an Air Support Control Party (ASCP) afloat and a Landing Force Air Support Control Unit (LFASCU) that shared responsibility for the coordination of air support. Before the air support function went ashore, the ASCP had authority to act on air support requests and the LFASCU was the subordinate unit. Ashore, the LFASCU became the senior unit and the ASCU became the subordinate unit. The Navy-Marine system placed ALPs at all levels of command, from the division down to the battalion. This represented a significant organizational difference between the two systems.[46]

The requirements of the tactical and operational situation drove the CAS organizational philosophy of the four services. The organizational structure, although changing in the Southwest Pacific from operation to operation, was a variant of the two organizational systems described above.

The Means and Effectiveness of Command and Control (C2):

The experiences of Lieutenant Colonel Keith B. McCutcheon during the Philippines Campaign serve as a good example of the methodology that created a command and control system that integrated the two CAS organizational structures and philosophies into a manageable system.

McCutcheon was the operations officer of Marine Air Group (MAG) 24, First Marine Aircraft Wing (1st MAW), in October of 1944. In early October, MAG 32 joined MAG 24 and moved to Bougainville.[47] McCutcheon learned that the Group would support Sixth Army on Luzon, Tenth Army Corps on Mindanao, and the 41st Division in Zamboango, and along with Fifth Air Force would provide CAS during the Philippines

---

[45] MeGee, 13.
[46] "An Evaluation of Air Operations Affecting the U.S. Marine Corps in World War II," II-11, II-12.
[47] Kevin L. Smith, "General Keith B. McCutcheon, USMC: A Career Overview–From the Dauntless to Da Nang," Masters thesis, (USMC, C&SC, 1999), 8.

Campaign.[48] He knew that MAG 24 was not ready to fly the CAS mission in combat and he suspected that the Army units were deficient as well.[49] McCutcheon gathered twenty-three documents of written material on the subject of CAS.[50] Very soon afterward he realized that the CAS material and doctrine then published was not standardized.[51] From his research, McCutcheon established a "doctrine." The CAS doctrine drew information out of SOPs, bulletins, memorandums, letters, FMs, intelligence summaries, and lessons learned from all the service branches.[52]

The doctrine he developed was based on the concept that CAS was an additional weapon of the ground commander and used against enemy forces and installations holding up the advance of allied forces.[53] McCutcheon went on to say that CAS was a weapon used at the discretion of the commander against targets that his organic weapons could not reach, or that ground commander could employ CAS in combination with other weapons in a coordinated attack.[54] He put a premium on timing and responsiveness of CAS. He wrote, "CAS should be immediately available and carried out deliberately, accurately and in coordination with other assigned units."[55]

McCutcheon's research revealed a structure described in GHQSWP SOP number 6. His solution was to develop a hybrid system that incorporated the best points of both the Marine and Army-Air Force systems.[56] He realized that the Navy and Marine system was wasteful at times.[57] He added to the Air Force control system the ALPs and manned them with pilots and placed them at the battalions of the supported divisions.[58] The Air Force and the Navy were not supportive of this concept and the Marines decided to man the ALPs, thinking it critical to achieve success.[59] The ALP was similar to modern

---

[48] McCutcheon, "Air Support Techniques," 24.
[49] McCutcheon, "Close Support Aviation," 120.
[50] Ibid., 136.
[51] Ibid., 121.
[52] Ibid., 136.
[53] Ibid., 122.
[54] Ibid.
[55] Ibid.
[56] McCutcheon, "Air Support Techniques," 24.
[57] Ibid., 24; Isely, 423.
[58] McCutcheon, "Close Air Support Aviation," 123; Taylor, 324.
[59] McCutcheon, "Close Air Support Aviation," 127; Isely, 423.

Tactical Air Control Parties. McCutcheon emphasized the need for unit integrity and familiarization with the terrain and the units they supported.[60] The bond established between individuals who knew each other built trust and understanding, which is what McCutcheon wanted to create.[61]

The organization and the communication system created a direct communication link between the front line battalions and the SAC.[62] Like the Navy and Marine system, when requests were forwarded from the battalion to the corps command post via the regiment and division, silence was consent and the request was acted upon unless modified by one of those commanders.[63]

Lieutenant Colonel McCutcheon set up a CAS school and prepared forty lectures, taught in five courses, in order to train all those involved in CAS operations.[64] Thirty-Seventh Army Division and MAG-24 scheduled and conducted a joint training exercise.[65] Pilots observed infantry attacks, terrain problems, and received instruction on infantry tactics.[66] The by-product of the instruction was a better understanding of the ground unit action, limitations on the pilots, and an appreciation of air limitations and capabilities by ground officers.[67] As a result of the training preparation, coordination, and integration, combat action in the Philippines Campaign saw Marine dive bombers dropping ordnance ever closer to the friendly lines as ground confidence in the aircraft went up.[68] The ALPs at the battalions were able to talk to the aircrews and see the targets themselves as they coached the pilot overhead onto the target.[69]

MAG 24 and MAG 32 proved the value of CAS by providing air alerts during daylight hours for most of a month to 1st Cavalry Division on its drive to Manila.[70] Air support acted as a screening force and flank guard of the 1st Cavalry Division as it

---

[60] McCutcheon, "Close Air Support Aviation," 124; Isely.
[61] McCutcheon, "Close Air Support Aviation," 132.
[62] McCutcheon, "Close Air Support Aviation," 124; Isely, 422.
[63] McCutcheon, "Close Air Support Aviation," 125.
[64] Ibid., 126, 133-35.
[65] McCutcheon, "Close Air Support Aviation," 127; Isely, 422.
[66] McCutcheon, "Close Air Support Aviation,"; Isely, 422; Taylor, 324.
[67] McCutcheon.
[68] Ibid., 128
[69] Ibid., 129.
[70] McCutcheon, "Close Air Support Aviation,"129; Taylor, 325.

moved forward.[71] The Marines provided ALPs to the battalion and regimental level and manned their teams with pilots while the Air Force supplied aviation observers to their ALPs.[72] McCutcheon reported that at times, the airfield was only 1-2 miles behind the front line of friendly troops, which added to the responsiveness of air support to a target called in by the battalions. It also gave the pilots and intelligence officers an opportunity to visit the front.[73]

McCutcheon's practical approach to training and coordination generated cooperation and trust between all the services' pilots and ground officers. The result was to increase knowledge and understanding of what was required to integrate CAS as an effective tactic into the battle plans from both the air and the ground perspective. It thus played a significant role in the success of the Philippines Campaign. The key to proficiency and control of CAS was communication, organization, training, coordination, and integration.

The Aircraft Basing Debate

The aircraft basing debate that was to take place during the Korean and Vietnam Wars was not experienced during World War II. The drive in the Southwest Pacific, hopping from island to island, was a campaign to secure air bases closer and closer to the Japanese home islands to conduct strategic attack and to secure the sea lines of communication. However, there were important facts to consider when basing aircraft for employment in CAS missions. The access and proximity of airfields mattered to tactical aircraft in World War II. It was a given that aviation would have to get close to the enemy, therefore the need to secure and maintain airfields on land and carriers at sea. The requirements for effective CAS were response time and effectiveness. Distance affected CAS response time. It also limited loiter time over the target.

The aircraft carrier could operate close to the objective area and remain there for a short time. However, the short deck of a carrier limited the takeoff ordnance weight of its aircraft. The result was that carrier aviation, although more responsive, was less

---

[71] McCutcheon, "Close Air Support Aviation," 129.
[72] McCutcheon, "Close Air Support Aviation," 132; Taylor, 324
[73] McCutcheon, "Close Air Support Aviation," 131; Taylor, 325.

efficient per sortie than land-based aircraft. Additionally, carriers, like airplanes, have limited endurance and must retire to replenish ordnance and fuel reserves.

During the Philippines Campaign, airstrips were as close as one or two miles from the front, which increased ordnance loads and efficiency per sortie, but also raised the level of risk. The problem was that airfields on land did not move and incurred a high risk when close to the contact zone. But land-based aircraft far from the front were less responsive.

Carrier-based aircraft required special training to support CAS operations, which was not received by all of the Navy squadrons. When these squadrons were not practiced in air support operations in ship-to-shore movements, they were not used in general support in close proximity to friendly troops. Carriers could move and operate close to the objective area but always ran the risk of being sunk, while land bases were fixed their commanders did not have to worry about sinking.

Summary

World War II, and especially the Philippines Campaign, developed a CAS doctrine that was well organized and functional. The system developed by Lieutenant Colonel McCutcheon was carried forward and used at Okinawa and was to be used during Operation Olympic, the planned invasion of Japan.[74]

Although never executed, Operation Olympic planners built on experience learned in the Philippines, Iwo Jima, and Okinawa, which laid the foundation for the Marine command and control organization in practice by 1946.[75]

The new organization consolidated the ADCC and the LFASCU under the single command of the Marine Air Control Group (MACG).[76] The battle experience in the Pacific pointed to the need for an organization to provide control of aircraft in both defensive and supporting missions.

The CAS lessons of World War II emphasized preparation, cooperation, coordination, integration, and the need for a standard CAS command and control

---

[74] Keith Barr McCutcheon, "Marine Air Control Group," (draft article dated 4 Sep 46), 3. McCutcheon Personal Collection (PC) #464, Box 4
[75] Ibid.
[76] Ibid.

doctrine. These lessons led to a comprehensive doctrine, but the bureaucracy failed to support the effort.[77] The result was that there was no agreed upon CAS doctrinal standard among the services by the time the Korean War started.

---

[77] McCutcheon, USMC, "Air Support Techniques", 24.

Chapter 3

CLOSE AIR SUPPORT IN THE KOREAN WAR

The fact that we have a suitable helicopter transport now in sight coupled with the answers arrived at during...participation in atomic exercises...leaves us with a sense of confidence.... The Marine Corps with [its] close air support and ...helicopters [will be] capable of following up an atomic attack with the most powerful assault punch possessed by any nation in the world.

Colonel Keith B. McCutcheon, Chief of Air Section, Marine Corps Equipment Board, quoting the Commandant of the Marine Corps

Introduction: Between World War II and the Korean War

The Marine Corps focused on surviving as a force and preserving its amphibious mission in the years between World War II and the Korean War. The Corps also continued to look at innovative concepts to improve efficiency in the conduct of its amphibious mission and its role as a force in readiness. The U.S. was demobilizing and the Marine Corps attempted to maintain capability and structure. The Corps' goal was to reorganize the Fleet Marine Force (FMF) into two divisions and two wings of approximately 100,000 men.[78] In 1945, the personnel end strength of the Marine Corps was 447,389 enlisted men and 37, 664 officers. By 1950, the USMC end strength had dropped to 67,025 enlisted men and 7,254 officers.[79] By the time the Korean War began the Marine Corps was but a shell of what it had been during WWII.

The Marine Commandant, General Alexander A. Vandergrift, appointed the Marine Corps Special Board to examine the relationship between nuclear weapons and amphibious operations.[80] The board reported to Vandergrift in December 1946 that the Corps would have to make radical changes to its amphibious doctrine and especially to its

---

[78] Alan R. Millett, *Semper Fidelis: the History of the United States Marine Corps* (Ontario Canada: The Free Press, 1991), 447.
[79] Ibid., 654.

ship-to-shore movement plan.[81] The answer to the nuclear threat in amphibious operations was a well-dispersed force. The Marine Corps pursued innovation in the helicopter. The Special Board examined vertical envelopment. A test squadron, HMX-1, was established in January 1948 and a tentative doctrine was written by November of that same year.[82]

Some Marine Corps CAS advocates perceived the helicopter as a threat to the existence of Marine fixed-wing aviation and the Marine CAS mission. Helicopter advocates such as Merrill Twining and Victor Krulak had to convince CAS advocates such as Brigadier General Vernon MeGee that the helicopter was not a threat to the Corps' fighter-bombers.[83] Lieutenant Colonel McCutcheon was instrumental in the development of tactics, techniques, and procedures for vertical envelopment. In August 1950, he experimented with helicopter weapon systems. He launched 3.5-inch rockets from a helicopter and developed helicopter bombing techniques.[84] These weapons systems and a camera tested by McCutcheon and HMX-1 proved difficult to build and sustain on early helicopters because of the vibration generated from the rotors and engines.[85]

The Marine Corps was the last service to procure helicopters.[86] The Army had experimented more extensively with guns mounted on helicopters in these early days of rotary-wing aviation. The armed helicopters must have caused some concern among Marine Corps fixed-wing aviation advocates and especially among CAS champions. Lieutenant Colonel McCutcheon was a prolific author by the end of the 1950s and even though he wrote several articles published in numerous professional journals, they never mentioned an armed helicopter variant. Two factors may have influenced this omission.

---

[80] Ibid., 453.
[81] Ibid.
[82] Ibid., 455.
[83] Ibid., 456.
[84] Kevin Smith, "General Keith B. McCutcheon, USMC: A Career Overview-From the Dauntless to Da Nang," (Marine Command and Staff, Masters of Military Studies Paper, 1999), 15.
[85] Keith B. McCutcheon, "Marine Corps Assault Aircraft Transports," (Presentation at the SAE Golden Anniversary Aeronautic Meeting, Hotel Statler, New York, NY, April 18-21, 1955), 1.
[86] McCutcheon, "Marine Corps Assault Aircraft Transports," 7.

First, early helicopters proved too unstable a platform for camera or gun. Second, a public debate over the arming of helicopters would have divided the Corps' aviation. A stormy debate between helicopter and CAS advocates would have created a hostile political atmosphere leading to internal divisions within Marine aviation at a time when the Marine Corps needed to present a unified philosophy.

The million-dollar helicopter program presented a direct fiscal threat to fixed wing CAS aviation in a time of shrinking budgets. The Navy decided not to count the dangerous and low status helicopters against the Corps aircraft numbers.[87] That, coupled with a decision to raise the developmental status of rotary wing aviation, may have saved the program and the future development of rotary wing CAS.

The Marine Corps was interested in other innovations that would improve it amphibious capability and readiness during this period between wars. It assigned Colonel Keith McCutcheon to the Bureau of Aeronautics (BuAer). As the department head of the guided missiles and pilot-less aircraft division, McCutcheon explored the development and use of these weapons from 1946 to 1949.

McCutcheon lectured to Marine Corps Reserve Officers in Philadelphia during February 1949. He said that, "If a third world war is to be fought this weapon (the guided missile) may usurp the place of the airplane."[88] He went on to say that

> ...push-button warfare is not with us yet, however guided missiles are just around the corner and we need to devote some serious thought to the [e]ffect of such new weapons on the Corps specialty, amphibious warfare.[89]

From a naval gunfire and artillery perspective, guided missiles were to provide a means to extend weapons effects beyond the possible ranges of conventional weapon

---

[87] Millett, *Semper Fidelis*, 466.
[88] Keith B. McCutcheon, "Guided Missiles," lecture, Marine Corps Volunteer Reserve Unit in Philadelphia, Pa., 9 February 1949 (Lieutenant Colonel Keith B. McCutcheon wrote draft papers entitled "Guided Missiles for Naval Operational Employment", "Guided Missiles", and "Automatically Guided Missiles". He wrote "Sign Post for the Future" published in the *Marine Corps Gazette*, March 1951, 35 no.3, 26-31, K.B. McCutcheon, PC#464, Box 5, Marine Corps University Archive (MCUA).
[89] Ibid.

systems of the day.[90] McCutcheon's model of the future, amphibious assault looked similar to, the past, only missiles and naval gunfire and pilot-less aircraft overhead would stand ready to provide fires and CAS. New command posts, and gadgets would keep the commander more up-to-date on the combat situation, which would provide the information necessary to commit the infantry to battle. McCutcheon thought that the infantry would still be necessary to take ground.[91]

During this period, the Army, like the Navy and Marine Corps, divided its effort between a few specific missiles and research and experimentation.[92] The Navy-Marine and the Army programs shared data and profited from each other's discoveries. The field was wide open for development. The objectives of each service's missile programs were so similar that each service benefited by the successful development achieved by the other. The guided missile committee since early 1945 had provided for the exchange of information essential to producing the best results on like projects.[93] The Marine Corps, as part of the Navy Department, benefited fiscally by its alignment with Naval aviation procurement and organization and its association with the Army project offices. One can only wonder why the services could cooperate in the development of new technologies but fail to arrive at a consensus on a joint air-ground doctrine during the same period.

The Marine Corps wanted to maintain its World War II missions and capabilities while its critics apparently wanted it stripped of its air arm and limited to regimental strength. The single most important act for the Air Force may have occurred when it became independent in 1947. The Marine Corps in the associated debates mobilized its political base to preserve the FMF, its air-ground team, and its amphibious mission as part of a Naval campaign. When the National Security Act of 1947 passed both houses and was signed by President Truman. Seemingly, the Marine Corps had won retention of its amphibious specialty and its force-in-readiness role.[94]

The Marines, having won a legal guarantee of continued existence, faced another

---

[90] Ibid.
[91] Ibid.
[92] Captain Teller, "Guided Missiles for Naval Operational Employment," (Naval War College Paper, n.d.), 13. (From the Keith B. McCutcheon personal papers PC#464, Box 5, MCUA).
[93] Teller, 13.

challenge: the battle for its share of the federal budget, which turned into an attack on the Marine Corps capability and structure. The Congress divided the Defense budget almost equally three ways, which left the total Marine budget in the 300 to 350 million-dollar range.[95] The budget cuts drove the Marine Corps to put off procurement of new equipment and to reduce training and manpower.[96] The Corps was a shell of its former strength and readiness. It performed limited exercises and testing of new weapons, but still conducted exercises on the east and west coasts.

FMF Pacific (FMFPAC) conducted four air-ground field exercises from May 1949 through June of 1950 and during the same period exercised airlift capabilities. The students of the Marine Command and Staff College viewed an amphibious demonstration in May 1950.[97] The Corps also authorized a series of CAS, command and control, communication, and amphibious exercises, which provided valuable air-ground lessons from 1948 to 1950. The Corps maintained a minimum state of readiness for embarkation and deployment for combat on ten days notice, in accordance with general policies, fleet directives, and operational war plans.[98]

Among items tested were the 75mm recoilless rifle, the 3.25 inch rocket, the CAS aircraft such as the Navy Douglas AD, and the first jet aircraft.[99] Marine fixed-wing aviation suffered by cuts in flying hours, maintaining World War II vintage aircraft, and competing with the rise of helicopter assault aviation.

The Marine Corps, like the other services, faced great challenges during the period between World War II and Korea. The national defense strategy focused on continental defense of the US, the European theater, and deterrence of the Soviet Union. The newly independent Air Force's mission focused on strategic warfare, the mission that

---

[94] Millett, *Semper Fidelis,* 464.
[95] Ibid., 466.
[96] Ibid.
[97] The Korean War Project, "An Evaluation of the Influence of the Marine Corps Forces on the Course of the Korean War, 4 August 1950 through 15 December 1950," vol. 2, appendix 80 "Pre-Korean Activity of FMFPAC" (This report is part of the Korean War Project at MCUA Box 1, folder 28).
[98] Marine Corps Board Study, *Evaluation of the Influence of the Marine Corps Forces on the Course of the Korean War*, 4 August 1950-15 December 1951, vol. 1 (Quantico, Va.1952), VI-A-1 and 2 (Korean War Project at MCUA Box 1, folder 27).
[99] Millett, *Semper Fidelis,* 466.

helped it gain independence from the Army. The Army was most concerned with the possibility of a major land war in Europe with the Soviet Union. Japan and the remainder of Asia became marginal to United States interests. It seemed that the chances of a small war were very remote. It seemed much more likely that the next conflict would be World War III.

In a strange way the Korean War may have saved the Marine Corps from extinction. By means of refined and pinpoint training, it focused limited assets on two primary missions and unknowingly prepared itself for the Korean War. The Marines' amphibious mission required an aviation arm expert in CAS as an integral part of the amphibious operational plan. Close air support concepts had not changed significantly since 1945, and CAS still provided a means to extend the range of naval gunfire and to reach targets in defilade.

However, there were differences of opinion among the armed services concerning the priority of CAS relative to other air missions. Additionally, none of the three major services could agree on a joint doctrine for air-ground operations. Only the Navy-Marine Corps team had revised their World War II doctrine by publishing the US Fleet (USF) publication series on naval warfare. The Air Force had decided to wait to publish a revised doctrine until the new service was firmly established. The Air Force also feared that a revision of FM 100-20 would cause a political controversy that might hinder service unification.[100]

The Korean War and Close Air Support Doctrine

Immediately following the outbreak of the Korean War, it was realized that the Army and some of the Air Force people knew little about the provisions of War Department Field Manual (FM) 31-35.

General Edwin J. Timberlake, Vice Commander, Fifth Air Force, Seoul Korea, October 1950

The CAS doctrinal differences that existed between the Navy-Marine Corps and

---

[100] Robert Frank Futrell, *Ideas, Concepts, and Doctrine: Basic Thinking in the United States Air Force 1907-1960*, vol. 1 (Maxwell AFB, AL: Air University Press, 1989), 366.

the Air Force during World War II persisted into the Korean War. The Army and the Air Force were still entrenched in the airpower experiences of the war in Europe five years earlier.[101] The Air Force and the Army looked to established doctrine by revising FM 100-20, *The Command and Employment of Airpower* (1943), and FM 31-35, *Air-Ground Operations* (1946), both of which were regarded as obsolete.

The Marines and the Navy largely maintained the same air philosophy they had championed during the war in the Southwest Pacific. The Navy and the Marines maintained a two-phased approach to amphibious assault and follow-on land operations. The Navy had published its perspective in US Fleet (USF) 6, *Amphibious Warfare Instructions*. The Army-Air Force and the Navy-Marine systems for tactical air support appeared to be in conflict, as they had during World War II.[102] Sections 63 and 66 of USF-6 established two primary principles: First, that unity of command and responsibility are necessary at the point of contact with the enemy; and second, the system of tactical air support of ground operations must be flexible, provide a simple and decisive procedure, and provide short notice employment of supporting aircraft.[103]

Marine and Navy air units were trained in the conduct of air operations under the command and control of a single air manager. The air commander was generally a Navy officer during amphibious assault when air forces were operating from fleet aircraft carriers. The responsibility for tactical air command shifted when aviation went ashore and began operating from land bases. The Tactical Air Commander then was generally the senior Marine aviator in the landing force. Marine aircraft wings operated in general or direct support of Marine divisions and not normally as attached units.[104]

The system of tactical air support established in USF-6 provided for the positive control of air assets. The central controlling agency at the headquarters of the force

---

[101] Allan R. Millett, "Korea, 1950-1953," in *Case Studies in the Development of Close Air Support*, ed., Benjamin Franklin Cooling (Washington, D.C.: OAFH USAF, 1990), 347.

[102] Futrell, *Ideas, Concepts, Doctrine 1907-1960*, vol. 1, 374.

[103] The Korean War Project, "An Evaluation of the Influence of the Marine Corps," Section IV-B-3 (This report is part of the Korean War Project at MCUA Box 1, folder 27).

[104] Ibid., Section IV-B-4 (This report is part of the Korean War Project at MCUA Box 1, folder 27).

commander executed positive control of air assets in the area of operations.[105] Subordinate agencies, down to the battalion, were connected by radio to the senior controlling agency so any battalion could request air support.[106] This process skipped extensive participation by intermediate commanders that characterized the Army-Air Force system. The Navy-Marine system implemented a by- exception rule and the request was processed unless it was vetoed by an intermediate commander.[107] This system provided the ground commander with a flexible and responsive method to receive CAS in support of his objectives.

It was recognized, after World War II, that the doctrine as written was not acceptable to all of the services and that it was inadequate. A standard joint air doctrine seemed achievable given the consensus concerning the need for a revised joint doctrine.[108] But the lessons of World War II faded quickly as political controversy and competition for money increased. The establishment of an independent Air Force, the service battles over roles and missions, along with a shrinking defense budget, fueled the controversy and distrust among the services. The Army and Air Force rejected proposals for revised joint doctrine, the "Joint Overseas Operations Manual," submitted by the Joint Operations review board to the JCS.[109] The Navy rejected a counter proposal made by the Army and Air Force, which was a revision of FM 31-5, *Landing Operations on Hostile Shores*.[110]

In 1948 the Army, looked to revise FM 31-35 and proposed the development of joint doctrine for airborne, tactical air support, air defense, and amphibious operations. The Marine Corps saw this as an attempt by the Army to wrest away a portion of the Marine Corps mission. The Air Force opposed the proposal based on its philosophy that airmen should develop and evaluate air tactics, techniques, and procedures.[111]

The services could not establish a joint doctrine before the Korean War. No service seemingly could overcome its distrust and suspicion of the others. By April 1950,

---

[105] Ibid.
[106] Millett, "Korea, 1950-1953," 352.
[107] Ibid.
[108] Futrell, *Ideas, Concepts, Doctrine*, 366.
[109] Ibid., 373.
[110] Ibid., 374.

the Air Force's Tactical Air Command and the Army Field Forces established a functional department theater level Joint Training Directive (JTD) as an expedient method to establish policy for air-ground operations.[112] But the JTD did not alter FM 31-35 and was only an elaboration of previous established doctrine. The Air Force saw the JTD as a threat to its control over mission priorities. The Army sensed that the directive failed to give the ground commander power over tactical air support.[113] On 1 September 1950, the Army Field Forces and Tactical Air Command went ahead and published the JTD as "the urgently needed amplification and revision of the principles, means, and procedures set forth in FM 31-35."[114] The JTD allocated control of the air-ground system to the regimental level and in special cases to the battalion.[115] The JTD changed little else and the services continued to pursue a joint doctrine for air-ground operations.

The Korean War unfolded in five phases. The initial defensive phase lasted from 25 June 1950 until 15 September. The offensive and exploitation phase lasted from 15 September to 6 November. The limited withdrawal and retrograde phase from Northeast Korea lasted from 6 November to 1 January 1951. And the stabilization phase has lasted to the present. The doctrinal employment and effectiveness of air forces during these phases of the war generated considerable controversy. Air Force concepts were challenged daily by the media, Congress, and the Army.

The employment of the Marine Corps changed over the course of the Korean War. The evolution of doctrinal shifts in the employment of Marine Corps aviation can be identified and characterized by three major operational events: Pusan Perimeter (initial defensive phase); Inchon to Seoul (the offensive-exploitation phase); and the Northeast Korean operations (limited withdraw-retrograde). In that regard, I will discuss the airpower employment priorities, the organization of CAS assets, the command and control system, and the aircraft basing debate.

---

[111] Ibid., 375.
[112] Millett, "Korea, 1950-1953," 350 (Also see Futrell, *Ideas, Concepts, Doctrine*, vol.1, 376-379, for a more detailed discussion concerning the JTD and follow on doctrinal guidance governing the functions of the armed forces).
[113] Millett, "Korea, 1950-1953," 350.
[114] Futrell, *Ideas, Concepts, Doctrine*, 377.
[115] Millett, "Korea, 1950-1953," 350.

Airpower Employment Priorities in Korea

The Korean War air priorities changed after the first few days of the war. The initial priorities set forth the establishment of air superiority over the peninsula followed by interdiction and CAS. All the services agreed that air superiority was the first step. This priority did not change after the completion of the air evacuation of Seoul four days into the war. But conflict and controversy soon arose over the priority of direct close air support of ground forces and the interdiction campaign in general support of ground forces.

The controversy arose from a few key factors. First, US leaders became concerned by the Air Force's easy achievement of air supremacy, while at the same time failing to stop the North Korean advance. Second, the speed with which the North Koreans advanced south in the face of their own lack of control of the sky over the battlefield was shocking. A third factor in the controversy came from Army commanders whose mounting criticism asserted the Air Force was not providing adequate air support to cover its initial withdrawal to defensive positions around Pusan.

The differences in service philosophy energized the debate. The Air Force initially saw the next objective priority as strategic attack and then interdiction of the enemy fielded force and lines of communications. It placed CAS last in priority as the least efficient mean of employing airpower in combat. The Air Force envisioned CAS used in direct support of ground operations only when the ground situation demanded it. It followed its battle-tested doctrine established in the European theater during World War II. But soon Air Force medium bombers ran out of important strategic targets.[116] The air planners then determined the location of the remaining strategic targets. But the North Koreans placed them in a "neutral" country politically out of reach of the Air Force.[117] President Truman constrained Far East Command from striking targets north

---

[116] "Command and Organization"(ASHAF-A, K168.04-1, Vol.1, Chapter 2, Section 1), 48.

[117] Appendix to the Congressional Record, "Lessons of the Air War in Korea," Extension of Remarks of the Honorable Melvin Price of Illinois in the House of Representatives, Thursday, December 7, 1950, 81st Congress, 2d Session, September 23, 1950-January 2, 1951, vol. 96, part 18, A7541. (Mr. Price cites for the record and the benefit of the

of the Yalu in Manchuria for fear of escalating the war into an overt conflict with China and the Soviet Union.[118]

The theater policy gave first priority to the establishment and maintenance of air supremacy over the Korean Peninsula. But the North Koreans never seriously challenged the United Nations (UN) forces for control of the air. They and the Chinese sent up MIG-15s in November 1950 to contest control of the air and to attack bombers only near the Manchurian border.[119] The introduction of MIG-15's into combat surprised the UN forces, but new US jet fighters quickly pushed them back across the Yalu River.[120]

The Air Force (having established air superiority from the start of the war) believed that the war would soon be well in hand. But the North Koreans and later the Chinese showed their mettle and cunning as an adversary by displaying extraordinary proficiency in the use of night movement and camouflage. The North Koreans also benefited from use of terrain and short lines of communication using foot and oxcart to supplement to limited rail and motor transport in supplying advancing forces.[121] Many observers in Washington and in the US Army's fielded forces wondered how the North Koreans could advance without air superiority and why the Air Force and Army were unable to stop the advance.

Royal Air Force Wing Commander P.G. Wykeham-Barnes addressed several overarching issues in his article on the Korean War and he focused mostly on Air issues. He wrote that the Air Force was not ready for the North Korean attack. The fighter squadrons stationed in Japan had not conducted exercises with the Army

---

members of the Congress for consideration an editorial written in the Legion Air Review by Lieutenant General Stratemeyer, Commander Far East Air Forces (FEAF).

[118] Department of the Air Force, *An Evaluation of the Effectiveness of the United States Air Force in The Korean Campaign*, Barcus Report, vol. I, "Command and Organization"(ASHAF-A, K168.04-1, Vol.1, Chapter 2, Section 1), 34.

[119] Department of the Air Force, *An Evaluation of the Effectiveness of the United States Air Force in The Korean Campaign*, Barcus Report, vol. III, "Operations and Tactics"(USAF Historical Archives ASI (hereafter sighted as: ASHAF-A) Maxwell, AL., K168.04-1, Vol.3, Chapter 1, Section 1), 6.

[120] Ibid.

[121] Barcus Report, vol. I, "Command and Organization," (ASHAF-A, K168.04-1, Vol.1, Chapter 2, Section 3) 45.

between 1945 and 1950. These FEAF squadrons stationed on Japanese soil had been training for the counter-air mission. They had not concentrated on the tactical support missions that were necessary to stop the advancing Communist invasion into South Korea.[122] Communication efforts seemed only to work well at home in static organizational and training environments, and never worked well under pressure of war. It seemed that the FEAF and the ground defense forces were not working as one machine, but as several individual and independent units. Obviously, this put United Nations forces at a disadvantage.[123]

General Timberlake confirmed these concerns in an interview conducted on 22 October 1950. He said that, before the initial phases of the conflict, the Air Force had tried to conduct a Joint Operations Center (JOC) exercise with the Eighth Army staff, but due to disagreement over the location of the JOC the Air Force and the Army dropped the training.[124]

On 21 May 1948, Air Force Bulletin No. 1 (AFB 1) published and listed the primary and collateral functions of the Air Force, as established by the JCS on 26 March 1948. AFB 1 listed close combat and logistical air support as number five in priority.[125] The FEAF mission responsibilities published just before the outbreak of the war included twenty-six mission tasks. Operational Instructions No. 1, Headquarter FEAF, listed CAS as the eleventh mission task.[126] Interestingly, the Barcus Report determined that it was not the responsibility of the Commanding General (CG), FEAF, to plan air

---

[122] P.G. Wykeham-Barnes, "Air Power Difficulties in the Korean," *Journal of the Royal United Service Institution* (Great Britain) May 1952. (Reproduced in *Military Review*, April 1953, 73-81), 74.
[123] Wykeham-Barnes, "Air Power Difficulties in the Korean," 75.
[124] General Edwin J. Timberlake, Vice Commander 5th Air Force, Transcript of USAF Evaluation Group Recorded Interview by Colonel J.B. Tipton, Operations, FEAF, 2. (Sterns Mission Report, Selected Interviews, USAF Historical Archives ASI (hereafter sighted as: ASHAF-A) Maxwell, Ala., K168.041-2, appendix H).
[125] Air Force Bulletin No. 1 (AFB 1), Department of the Air Force, Washington, D.C., 21 May 1948, 8. (See Korean Evaluation Project, "Report on Air Operations" Barcus Mission Report, Supporting Letters, ASHAF-A, K168.041, vol. 20).
[126] AFB-1, (ASHAF-A, Maxwell, Ala., K168.04-1, Vol.1, Chapter 1, Section 2), 8.

operations incident to Korea beyond air transport operations.[127] The FEAF subordinate units stressed air defense training as their primary mission.[128]

General Timberlake in his interview to the Sterns Commission addressed this conundrum:

> We had a primary mission – Air Defense. Along about last January (1950) we were given a secondary mission of air-ground cooperation. The Army at that time was switching over from an occupation mission to a combat mission…and training was limited to company and battalion level Tactical Air Control Party (TACP) training. We had in addition to our main mission, various missions, one of which was an evacuation of American Nationals from Korea, known as Operations Plan 4.[129]

On 27 June 1950, President Truman authorized aggressive action against the North Koreans. The FEAF completed the civil evacuation on 28 June. The President authorized the FEAF to cross the 38th parallel the next day. On 30 June, the President directed the commitment of ground forces and the Eighth Army moved the 24th Division to Pusan.[130] From the start of hostilities the FEAF had the mission of interdiction of North Korean Forces and the close support of the Republic of Korea (ROK) army as they withdrew past Seoul to Pusan.[131]

The overall action during the Korean War developed into five phases and during each phase the air priorities changed depending on the tactical and operational situation. Air Superiority remained the overarching priority and was always a consideration in planning. But the air priority battle shifted between interdiction and CAS throughout the remainder of the War.[132]

During the initial defensive phase, the General Headquarter Staff, Far East Command (GHQFEC), placed CAS next in priority behind the establishment of air supremacy over Korea.[133] The Barcus commission reported that during the first six weeks of the war the FEAF placed an extraordinary emphasis on the general and direct

---

[127] Ibid., 10.
[128] Ibid.
[129] Timberlake, interview, ASHAF-A, K168.041-2, appendix H, 1-3.
[130] Timberlake, interview and chronology, ASHAF-A, K168.041-2, appendix H, 1-3.
[131] "Command and Organization"(ASHAF-A, K168.04-1, Vol.1, Chapter 2, Section 1), 47-48.
[132] Ibid., 46.
[133] Ibid., 36.

support of ground operations.[134] The GHQFEC ordered the FEAF to halt the enemy's advance and help secure the defensive line around Pusan.[135] The plan was designed to buy time to build up Eighth Army and prepare for amphibious operations to provide direct support to withdrawing ROK forces.[136] FEAF aircraft provided tactical support to the ROK in the following priorities: attacking the advancing enemy tanks, artillery, and military convoys, followed by supply dumps, bridges, and targets of opportunity.[137]

Marine aviation entered combat on 3 August flying from escort carriers (CVE) and from Itazuka, Japan.[138] The Marines landed at Pusan and Masan on 4 August and entered the defensive line on the Pusan perimeter.[139] The 1st MAW entered the Korean theater and was attached to Fifth Air Force, while the Marine Brigade (later 1st Marine Division) was attached to Tenth Corps.[140] Sea-based Marine squadrons remained under the direction of the Navy.[141] The Marines then established their air control system, and FEAF assigned two land-based Marine air support squadrons to support the Marine Brigade.[142]

The 1st Marine Brigade deployed to Korea below its authorized organizational wartime allowance.[143] The Brigade was committed to combat with two companies per infantry battalion, vice the normal three.[144] The Brigade's artillery battalion only had four howitzers per battery instead of the normal six.[145] The Marines arrived with one battalion of 105mm howitzers in direct support.[146] Artillery was limited throughout the theater with little heavy or medium guns available to reinforce the Marine number of

---

[134] Ibid., 37.
[135] Ibid., 44-45.
[136] Ibid., 47.
[137] Ibid.
[138] Timberlake, interview, 8.
[139] Ibid.
[140] The Korean War Project, "An Evaluation of the Influence of the Marine Corps," Section IV-B-9 (MCUA Box 1, folder 27).
[141] Ibid., Section IV-B-9-11 (MCUA Box 1, folder 27).
[142] Timberlake, (ASHAF-A, K168.041-2, appendix H) Command and Organization" (ASHAF-A, K168.04-1, Vol.1, Chapter 2, Section 1), 6-8.
[143] The Korean War Project, "An Evaluation of the Influence of the Marine Corps," Section II-A-16 (MCUA Box 1, folder 27).
[144] Ibid.
[145] Ibid.

light guns.[147] Naval gunfire could not support the Marines either because of range limitations.[148] Eighth Army's heavy Corps artillery, virtually non-existent in July and August 1950, did not reach adequate strength until 1951.[149] By September 1950, the Marines established the 1st Marine Division in Korea with First Marines, Fifth Marines, and Seventh Marines (infantry regiments), and Eleventh Marines the division's artillery regiment.[150] Eleventh Marines after September 1950 consisted of five battalions; First, Second, Third, Fourth, and reinforced by the Ninety-sixth Field Artillery Battalion, US Army.[151]

The Marine Corps often argued that it required its own aviation to support amphibious operations.[152] Amphibious forces lack significant artillery support during amphibious operations and rely on Naval gunfire, carrier air, Marine air, and Air Force for fire support.[153] The Army in comparison during normal land operations generates massed fire support from the field artillery organized at the corps and division level.[154] However, in Korea, Eighth Army experienced weakness in its field artillery by September 1950 it was reinforced initially with five battalions of heavy gun battalions from the United States.[155]

Normal principles employed to achieve effective fire support in land warfare operations were equally true for amphibious operations.[156] But in amphibious operations before the establishment of the beachhead artillery was not generally available. A heavy reliance on air support was required to maintain the momentum of

---

[146] Ibid.
[147] Millett, "Korea, 1950-1953," 358.
[148] The Korean War Project, "An Evaluation of the Influence of the Marine Corps," Section II-A-16 (MCUA Box 1, folder 27).
[149] Millett, "Korea, 1950-1953," 358.
[150] The Korean War Project, "An Evaluation of the Influence of the Marine Corps," Section II-B-37 (MCUA Box 1, folder 27).
[151] Ibid.
[152] William W. Momyer, *Airpower in Three Wars (WWII, Korea, Vietnam)* (Washington, D.C., Department of the United States Air Force), 59.
[153] Ibid.
[154] Ibid.
[155] Millett, "Korea, 1950-1953," 358.
[156] The Korean War Project, "An Evaluation of the Influence of the Marine Corps," Section IV-C-1 (MCUA Box 1, folder 27).

the assault.[157] Once the advancing forces exceeded the limited range of naval gunfire was it became necessary to bring artillery ashore and coordinate its fires with aviation fires. The effectiveness of fire support and its coordination with other arms and forces was dependant on adequate, reliable communication and the employment of flexible supporting arms.[158] The Marines practiced coordination and cooperation among the Marine supporting arms organizations as well as between the other services helped connect the Navy, to the Army and Air Force.

Major General Edward A. Craig, the Commanding General of the 1st Provisional Marine Brigade, considered the weakness of the available artillery and the need to coordinate the employment of weapons talked with General MacArthur upon arriving in theater.[159] He mentioned to General MacArthur the fact that the Marine Brigade and the Marine Aircraft Wing before the war worked together on a daily basis at Camp Pendleton.[160] General Craig requested that Marine aviation support the brigade if at any time the Marines were committed to combat, in view of the fact that the Marines had trained together and could get positive results.[161] He explained to MacArthur that if the Marines used Air Force support, they would be using people who had not operated with them and who could not give them proper support on the ground.[162] General MacArthur agreed and Marine aviation supported the Marine Brigade throughout the campaign in the south.

The addition of Navy and Marine aviation enabled the UN forces to break out and FEAF devoted some of the air effort to the interdiction of major enemy ground forces and supplies moving south to reinforce the enemy's position.[163] By 15 August,

---

[157] Ibid.
[158] Ibid., IV-C-2.
[159] Major General Edward A. Craig, 1st Provisional Marine Brigade and assistant Commanding General 1st Marine Division, Interview transcript, 8 May 1951, 41 (Historical Division, Headquarters, U.S. Marine Corps (USMCHD), The Pusan Perimeter through Pohang Commitment, CD-ROM collection of Korean War Historical Documents, CD No.14 of 24).
[160] Ibid.
[161] Ibid.
[162] Ibid.
[163] "Command and Organization"(ASHAF-A, K168.04-1, Vol.1, Chapter 2, Section 1), 37.

sufficient UN forces had arrived in theater that the ground situation around Pusan had stabilized and GHQFEC considered a shift in priority to emphasize and interdiction campaign.[164]

Captain F. Foxworth, a pilot with Marine Fighter Squadron (VMF) 311, described a mission he flew over the Pusan Perimeter in an interview to a member of the Marine 1st Provisional Historical Platoon.[165] The Air Force controllers described the missions from Pusan as CAS, he said. But, these missions were not like the Marine concept of CAS. Foxworth worked with the "Mosquitoes" (Air Force airborne forward controllers). On this occasion, the Mosquito went off station when he arrived and simply passed the word that three nearby towns were full of enemy soldiers.[166] Such methods were at times situation driven but were not described as very helpful to troops on the front line.

First Lieutenant A.D. Antone (VMF-311) echoed Foxworth's comments. Antone reported working CAS missions with Mosquito controllers.[167] When he checked in with the Mosquito on a CAS mission the Mosquito said, "This is a CAS, repeat CAS, own troops are one and a half miles away."[168] These missions, in terms of Marine doctrine, were interdiction or deep support missions. These missions seemed to indicate that the FEAF conducted an interdiction campaign from the beginning of the war. They also indicate that the definition of CAS differed between services.

United Nations offensive operations began on 15 September 1950 and signaled the beginning of phase two.[169] The priority of the air effort began to shift again during this phase of the Korean Campaign. Tactical air support in the form of transportation and airlift grew in importance.[170] The need for CAS diminished with the offensive

---

[164] Ibid.
[165] Captain F. Foxworth, VMF-311, 1st Marine Aircraft Wing, FMF, interviewed by Marine 1st Historical Platoon, 23 January 1951 (USMCHD, CD No.14 of 24).
[166] Ibid.
[167] First Lieutenant A.D. Antone, VMF-311, 1st Marine Aircraft Wing, FMF, interviewed by Marine 1st Historical Platoon, 23 January 1951 (USMCHD, CD No.14 of 24).
[168] Ibid.
[169] "Command and Organization"(ASHAF-A, K168.04-1, Vol.1, Chapter 2, Section 1), 37.
[170] Ibid., 38.

successes gained by the Marines and Tenth Corps at the Inchon landing.[171] The subsequent breakout from Inchon, push to Seoul, and the linkup of ground forces from the Pusan Perimeter near Seoul favored a shift in priority to an aerial interdiction campaign. Elements of the North Korean Army dissolved in place under the coordinated fires of UN forces.[172] The UN forces exploited and pursued the remnants of the North Korean Army north past the 38th parallel and conducted an operational pause at the 38th parallel in early October 1950.[173]

The Truman administration authorized GHQFEC to conduct offensive ground operations north of the 38th parallel to pursue the withdrawing North Korean Army.[174] The resistance offered by the North Koreans as they withdrew north was light. Request for CAS increased, but the weight of the air effort continued to focus on armed reconnaissance and interdiction.[175] The air priorities did not change at this time.[176] The highlight of this phase of the campaign was the unopposed landing by UN forces at Wonsan. The Tenth Corps, the 1st Marine Division, and the US Seventh Infantry Division landed at Wonsan and Iwon and pursued the enemy north toward the Manchurian border.[177] Days later, the ROK First Corps followed the coastal routes north toward Chongjin.[178] The 1st Marine Division marched toward Hamhung, Koto-ri, and the Chosin Reservoir, while the Seventh Division marched inland toward Pujon Reservoir.[179]

The third phase of the Korean War commenced when the Chinese entered the war. The Eighth Army attempted to consolidate its lines north of Poyongyang in early November. The Eighth Army conducted a limited withdrawal, breaking contact with the enemy north of Chingchon in late November. The requirement for CAS went up at the same time that the Chinese sent MIGs south of the Yalu. The priorities remained

---

[171] Ibid., 38.
[172] Ibid., 37.
[173] Ibid., 37.
[174] Ibid., 38.
[175] Ibid., 38.
[176] Ibid., 38.
[177] Robert F. Futrell, *The United States Air Force in Korea 1950-1953* (Air Force History and Museums Program 2000), 213-214.
[178] Ibid., 214.

the same, however, due to an increase in available air assets. The FEAF was then able to support the additional requirements without affecting the commitment to interdiction and armed reconnaissance.[180]

Tenth Corps and the Marines in northeast Korea made significant progress against light resistance until the end of November, reducing the necessity for CAS. Tenth Corps was "air rich" in that it received help from the 1st MAW and Navy Task Force 77, in addition to Fifth Air Force support.[181]

Surprisingly, the armed reconnaissance and interdiction missions failed to detect the Chinese communists crossing the Yalu during the last week of November and the first week of December.[182] The Chinese attack flanked the Eighth Army and centered on the 1st Marine Division and Tenth Corps, signaling the beginning of the fourth phase. Heavy attacks by the Chinese cut off elements of the UN forces in the Chosin Reservoir sector of the UN line. The air priorities rapidly changed to emphasize air support of ground forces.[183] Air and artillery provided the necessary support for the 1st Marine Division to withdraw with all its equipment and men through Koto-ri and Hanghung to Wosan.[184]

The UN Forces reorganized and redeployed, establishing a defensive line near the 38th parallel north of Seoul. The battle-line stabilized near the 38th parallel. The air priorities changed for short periods as the tactical and operational situation changed on the ground.[185]

Service Air Philosophies in Korea

The way the services viewed the prioritization of air missions displayed a significant difference in air philosophy during the Korean War. The Air Force saw the best method

---

[179] Ibid.
[180] "Command and Organization" (ASHAF-A, K168.04-1, Vol.1, Chapter 2, Section 1), 38.
[181] Futrell, *The United States Air Force in Korea 1950-1953*, 255.
[182] "Command and Organization" (ASHAF-A, K168.04-1, Vol.1, Chapter 2, Section 1), 39.
[183] Ibid.
[184] Ibid.

of applying airpower as a concentration of effort focusing on a decisive point. The Air Force in Korea remained convinced that the focus of the air effort should be on interdiction and strategic attack. The Air Force's interdiction campaign economized the use of air forces. The Air Force was reluctant to water down the interdiction campaign by siphoning off air assets for ostensibly less efficient CAS missions. It desired to provide general support to ground forces and react to requests for close air support. Additionally, the Air Force offered to provide direct support on an as required basis by diverting other missions to the CAS role.

The air priorities, organization, and process required to employ this type system and provide responsive CAS presupposes a near perfect world. The system that always places its priorities on interdiction and strategic attack ahead of CAS would require the following: 1) aircraft load-out to be generic to support both CAS and interdiction missions, and that the ordnance provided be equally effective in both roles; 2) the communication system between control agencies, aircraft, and ground units would need to operate at near 100% efficiency and be redundant; 3) control agencies would need near perfect information about the aircraft and its status, configuration, and mission; and 4) the aircraft and pilot must be able to divert to a CAS mission from another pre-briefed mission.

The Marine priorities centered on Marine air support of the 1st Marine Division. The Marines did not have the capability or the authority to drive the theater air priorities to CAS. The authority to determine the air priority in Korea rested with the FEAF and the GHQFEC. The 1st MAW operated as an integrated part of FMF in Korea and was therefore able to provide direct support to the 1st Marine Provisional Brigade. The Marine aviation units operated in support of the Brigade as the highest priority and supported UN forces as a lower priority. The Marines' doctrine and available assets drove them to believe in a more "balanced" approach to air prioritization. The Marines and the Navy considered interdiction and CAS as requiring equal attention.

---

[185] "Command and Organization" (ASHAF-A, K168.04-1, Vol.1, Chapter 2, Section 1), 40.

The Army emphasized CAS in a memorandum to the Chief of staff of the Air Force. General Mark Clark outlined the Army Fielded Forces opinion on CAS. He stated in November 1950,

> There is an indispensable requirement for adequate, effective air support for ground operations at all times. This requirement is currently not being met satisfactorily. This requirement should be met at the earliest possible date under conditions and on a minimum scale as follows: 1) For overseas provision of one (1) fighter bomber group per Army Division, and one (1) reconnaissance group per field army, increased to two (2) upon full mobilization. 2) For the zone of interior, provision one fighter-bomber group per two army divisions and one reconnaissance group for the present troop basis of seven divisions. 3) The Army tactical commander, down to include the corps level in some instances, should exercise operational control of close air support units engaged in providing reconnaissance and fire support to the ground operations.[186]

General Clark's memorandum reflected the Army's request to raise the priority of CAS in the Korean Theater. The Clark memorandum also supported General Almonds' (the Tenth Corps Commanding General) position on CAS in Korea and the Army's desire to attach aviation to the divisions.

During the initial phases of the war through the Inchon landing and the pursuit of the enemy, the CAS controversy persisted. The controversy developed over the priority and efficiency of Air Force CAS as an air mission task in support of ground operations. The priority of CAS during the Korean War was not the problem so much as it was an organizational problem and the perceived utility of CAS. The lack of communication between air and ground units, the exact location of frontline units, and the massing of enemy troops at critical points along the battle-line contributed to the FEAF's perceived inability to provide adequate CAS in direct support of ground units.[187]

It was clear that from the standpoint of mission, doctrine, and tradition the Marines and the Navy had established, tested, and improved a system for air-ground operations

---

[186] General Mark Clark, General Army Fielded Forces, Memorandum to Chief of Staff, Department of the Army, subject: Tactical Air Support of Ground Forces, Tab C, enclosure 3, November 1950 (Army TacAir Memorandum, Tactical Air Support for Ground Forces Memo, 13 September, 1951, http://carlisle-www.army.mil/cgi-bin/usamhi/DL/).

[187] "Command and Organization"(ASHAF-A, K168.04-1, Vol.1, Chapter 2, Section 1), 40.

over the several years since World War II. The Marines still considered the primary purpose of tactical aviation to be support of ground troops. They trained extensively and developed aviation employment techniques to support that mission before the Korean War.[188] These factors coupled with special conditions specific to the Korean War and its timing provided the Marine Corps with a chance to prove its capability in CAS.

See diagram of the two CAS control systems in Korea: Figure 3, the Joint Policy Agreement for Control of Aircraft Operating over Korea; Figure 4, the Navy-Marine Control System Close Air Support Architecture during Amphibious operations Korea; Figure 5, Army-Air Force Control System Close Air Support Architecture during operations in Korea; Figure 6, The Navy-Marine Request Procedures Korea; Figure 7, The Navy-Marine Execution Procedures Korea; Figure 8, The Army-Air Force Request Procedures Korea; and Figure 9, The Army-Air Force Execution Procedures Korea.

Organization of CAS Assets

On 8 July 1950, GHQFEC assigned command and operational control of all aircraft operating in the execution of FEAF missions in Korea.[189] The FEAF delegated to Fifth Air Force controlling authority over all tactical air support operations in Korea for most of the war.[190] The only exception to Fifth Air Force's authority occurred during the Inchon amphibious operations. The US Naval Forces Far East (USNF-FE) maintained command and operational control of all aircraft over water.[191] During the Inchon amphibious operations USNF-FE Joint exercised air command and operational control over land in the amphibious objective area in addition to its normal operational tasking.[192]

---

[188] The Korean War Project, "An Evaluation of the Influence of the Marine Corps", vol. 1, Section IV-B-2 (MCUA Box 1, folder 27).

[189] Major General Edward M. Almond, GHQFEC, Chief of Staff, by command of General MacArthur, to Commander, United States Naval Forces Far East (NAVFE), and Commanding General, Far East Air Forces, letter, subject: Coordination of the Air Effort of Far East air Forces and United States Naval Forces Far East, AG370.2, 8 July 1950 ("Korean Evaluation Project: Report on Air Operations" (Barcus Mission), Command Relations, Appendix II, vol. 1 ASHAF-AK168.041-2).

[190] The Korean War Project, "An Evaluation of the Influence of the Marine Corps", vol. 1, Section IV-B-9 (MCUA Box 1, folder 27).

[191] Almond, GHQFEC, Chief of Staff, letter, 8 July 1950 (ASHAF-AK168.041-2).

[192] The Korean War Project, "An Evaluation of the Influence of the Marine Corps," vol. 1, Section IV-B-9 (MCUA Box 1, folder 27).

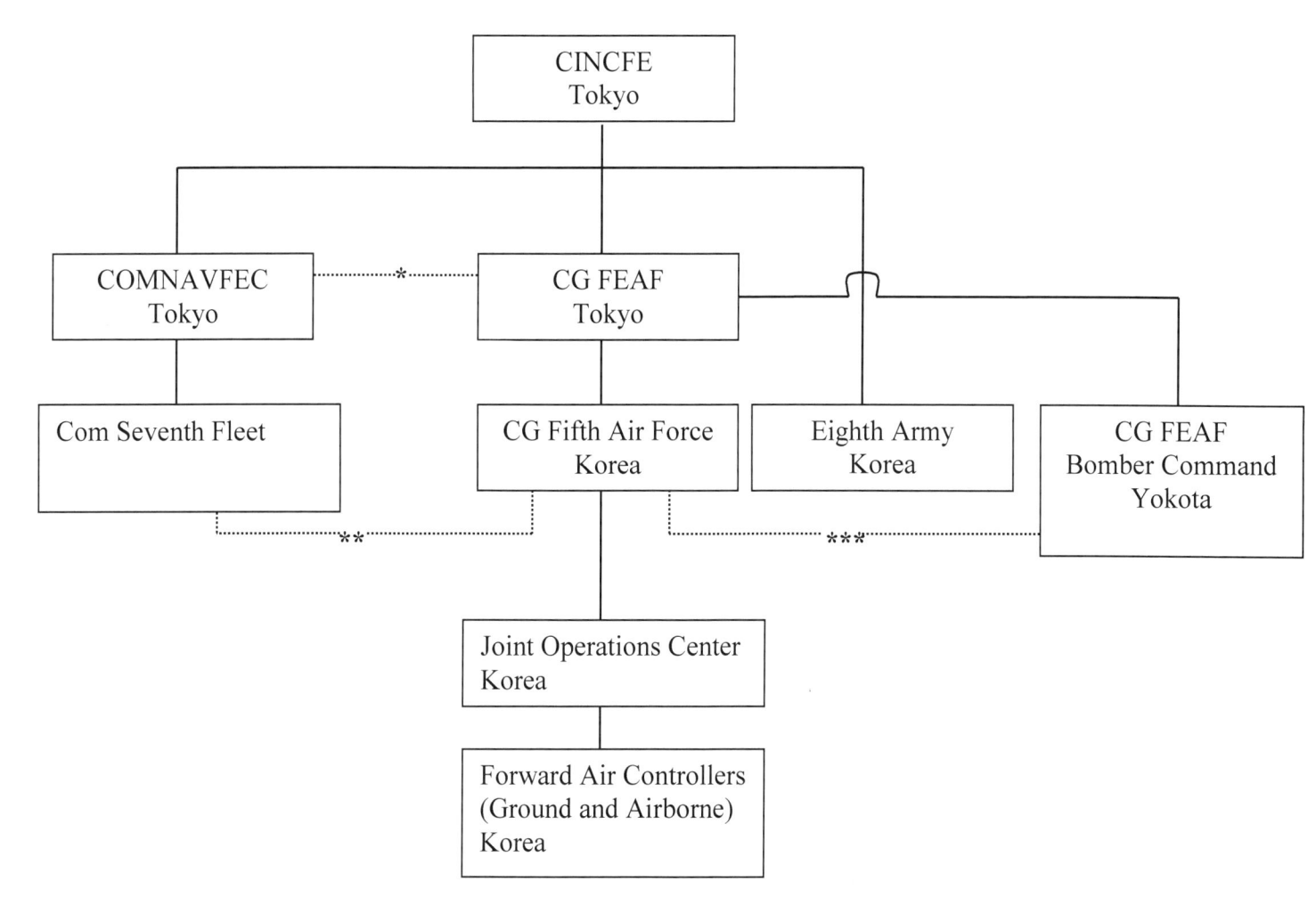

```
                          ┌─────────────┐
                          │   CINCFE    │
                          │    Tokyo    │
                          └──────┬──────┘
              ┌──────────────────┼──────────────────────────────┐
      ┌───────┴──────┐    ┌──────┴──────┐                       │
      │  COMNAVFEC   │····*····│  CG FEAF │                     │
      │    Tokyo     │    │    Tokyo    │                       │
      └───────┬──────┘    └──────┬──────┘                       │
              │          ┌───────┼────────────┐                 │
    ┌─────────┴──────┐ ┌─┴───────────┐ ┌──────┴──────┐  ┌───────┴────────┐
    │Com Seventh Fleet│ │CG Fifth Air │ │ Eighth Army │  │   CG FEAF      │
    │                 │ │Force Korea  │ │   Korea     │  │Bomber Command  │
    │                 │ │             │ │             │  │   Yokota       │
    └─────────────────┘ └──────┬──────┘ └─────────────┘  └────────────────┘
                ············**·······           ·······***·······
                               │
                        ┌──────┴──────────┐
                        │Joint Operations │
                        │ Center Korea    │
                        └──────┬──────────┘
                        ┌──────┴──────────┐
                        │Forward Air      │
                        │Controllers      │
                        │(Ground and      │
                        │ Airborne) Korea │
                        └─────────────────┘
```

* FEAF " Coordination Control"

** FEAF (Fifth Air Force) operational control of 1st Marine Aircraft Wing's land based assets and carrier based Marine air when operating over land in support of Army and Marine ground forces.

*** Fifth Air Force authority for coordination of bomber strikes with all other forces and functions.

(Reminder: Tenth Corps not listed here operated as an independent Corps for the first few months of the war with the 1st Marine Division attached in support. After January 1951, Tenth Corp and the Marine operated under Eighth Army.)

Source W. Momyer, *Airpower in Three wars*

Figure 3. Agreement for Control of Aircraft Operating over Korea

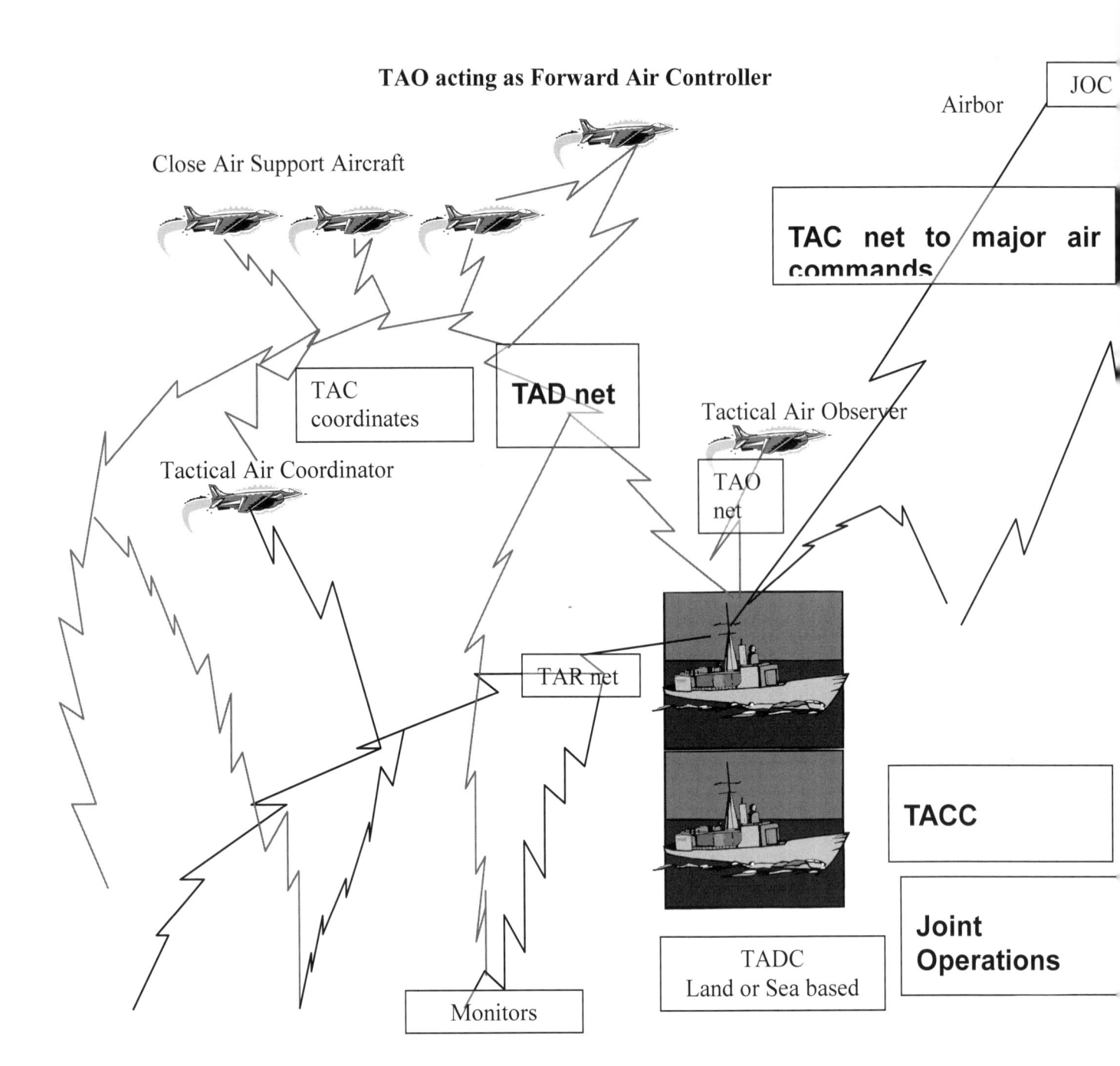

TAO acting as Forward Air Controller

Close Air Support Aircraft

TAC coordinates

TAD net

Tactical Air Observer

TAO net

Airbor... JOC

TAC net to major air commands

Tactical Air Coordinator

TAR net

TADC Land or Sea based

TACC

Joint Operations

Monitors

50

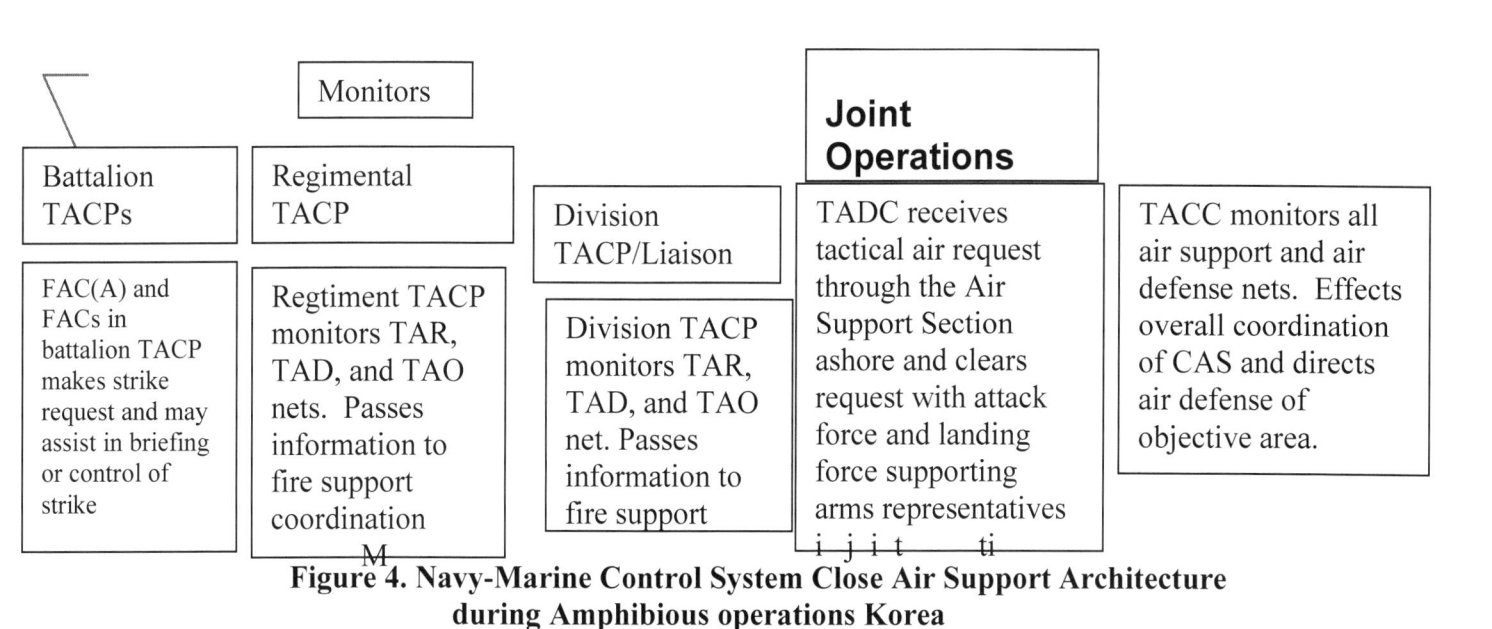

Battalion TACPs	Regimental TACP (Monitors)	Division TACP/Liaison	Joint Operations	
FAC(A) and FACs in battalion TACP makes strike request and may assist in briefing or control of strike	Regtiment TACP monitors TAR, TAD, and TAO nets. Passes information to fire support coordination	Division TACP monitors TAR, TAD, and TAO net. Passes information to fire support	TADC receives tactical air request through the Air Support Section ashore and clears request with attack force and landing force supporting arms representatives	TACC monitors all air support and air defense nets. Effects overall coordination of CAS and directs air defense of objective area.

Figure 4. Navy-Marine Control System Close Air Support Architecture during Amphibious operations Korea

Close Air Support Aircraft

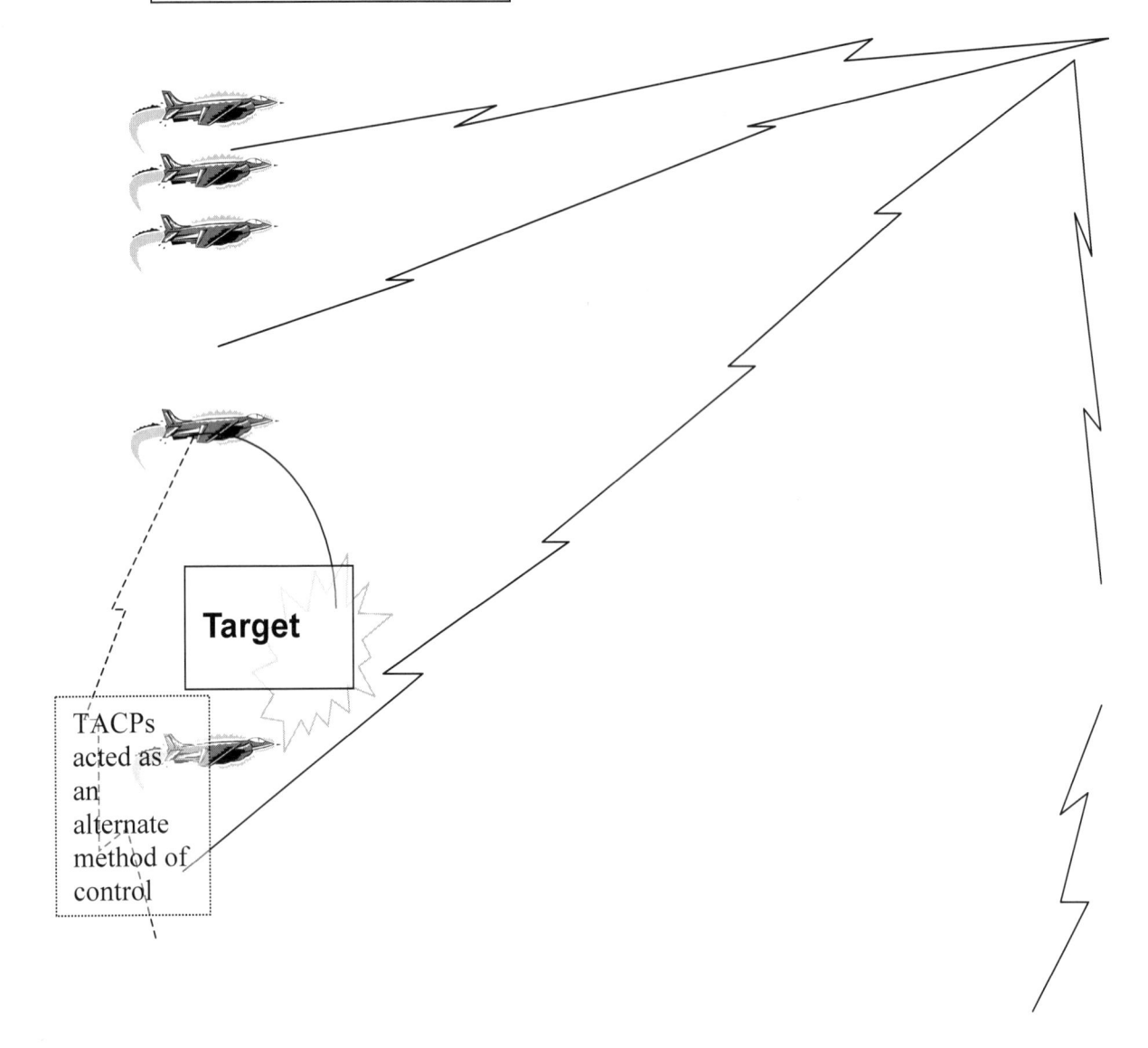

Forward Air Controller Airborne (T-6 Mosquitos in role)

CAS coordin with controll preferre method control

Target

TACPs acted as an alternate method of control

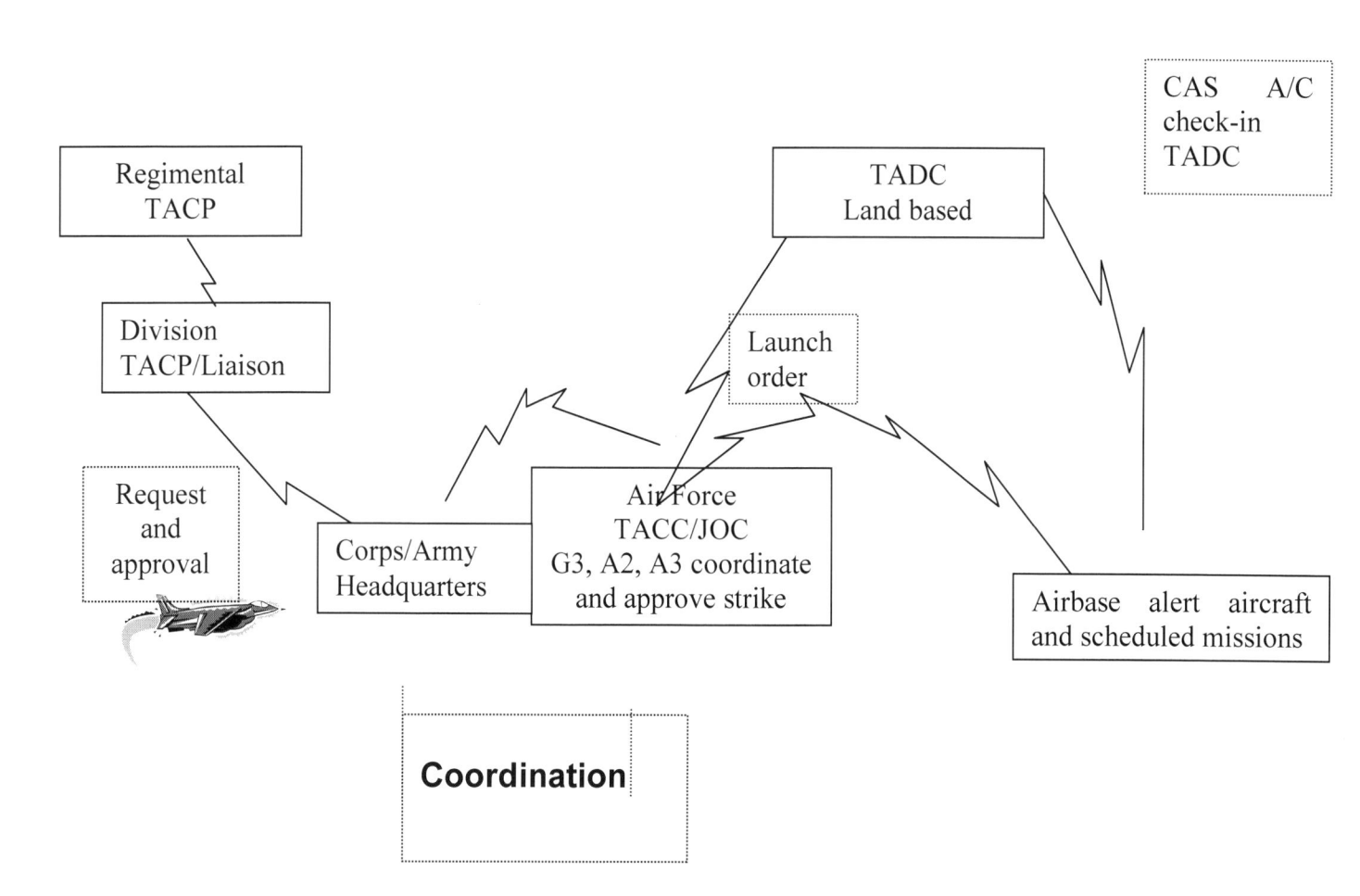

Figure 5. Army-Air Force Control System Close Air Support Architecture during operations in Korea

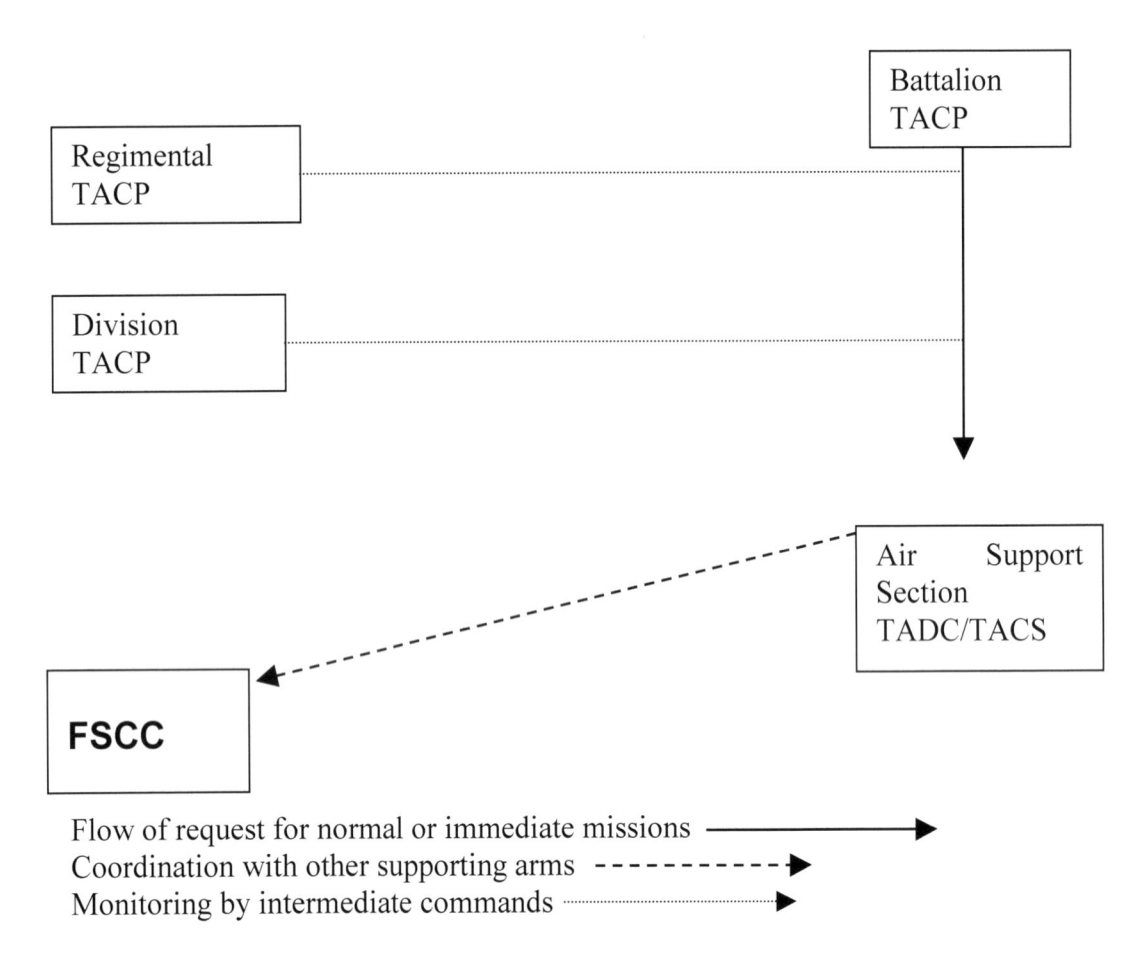

```
┌─────────────┐                    ┌─────────────┐
│ Regimental  │....................│ Battalion   │
│ TACP        │                    │ TACP        │
└─────────────┘                    └─────────────┘
                                          │
┌─────────────┐                           │
│ Division    │...........................│
│ TACP        │                           │
└─────────────┘                           │
                                          ▼
                                   ┌─────────────┐
                                   │ Air Support │
                        ┌ ─ ─ ─ ─ ─│ Section     │
                        │          │ TADC/TACS   │
                        ▼          └─────────────┘
┌─────────────┐
│ **FSCC**    │
└─────────────┘
```

Flow of request for normal or immediate missions ──────────▶
Coordination with other supporting arms ─ ─ ─ ─ ─ ─▶
Monitoring by intermediate commands ·················▶

Source: V.E. McGee, "Tactical Air Support of Ground Forces," *Marine Corps Gazette*, December 1955, 15.

Figure 6. Navy-Marine Request System Korea

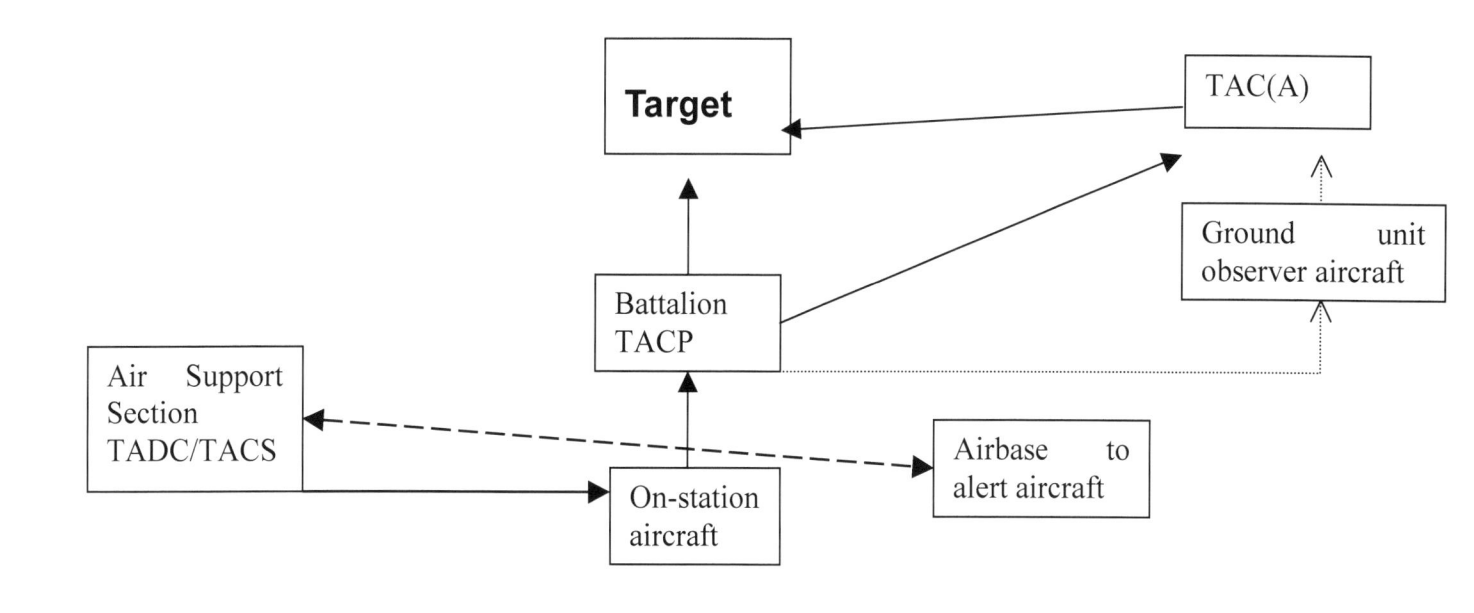

Control follows this line ⟶
Indicates alternate source of aircraft – – –▶
Indicated alternate source of target information ┄┄┄>

Source: V.E. McGee, "Tactical Air Support of Ground Forces," *Marine Corps Gazette*, December 1955, 15.

Figure 7. Navy-Marine Execution Procedure Korea

Flow of request for preplanned missions - - - - - ▶

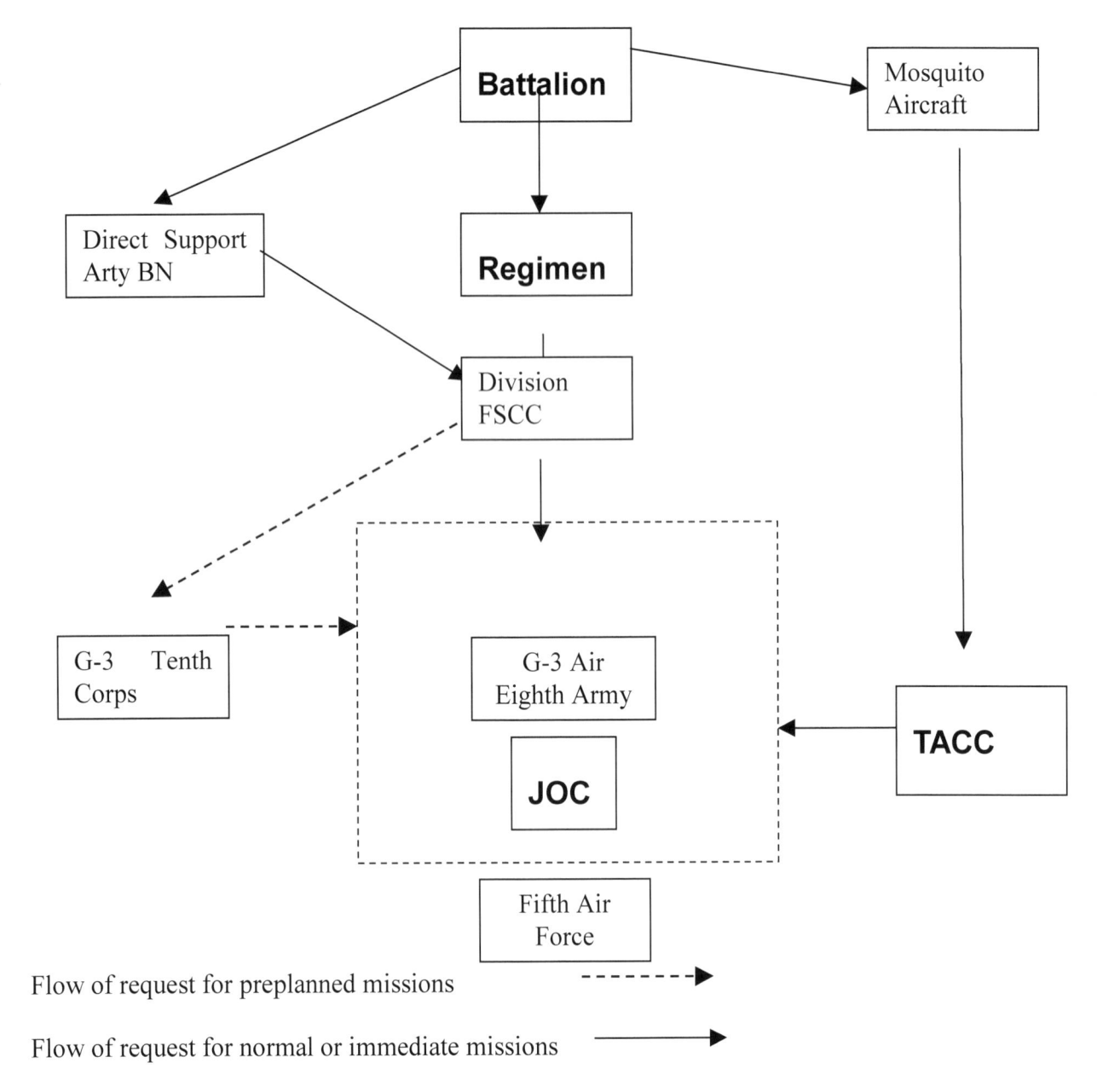

Flow of request for normal or immediate missions ⎯⎯⎯▶

Source: V.E. MeGee, "Tactical Air Support of Ground Forces," *Marine Corps Gazette*, December 1955, 15.

Figure 8. Army-Air Force Request Procedure Korea

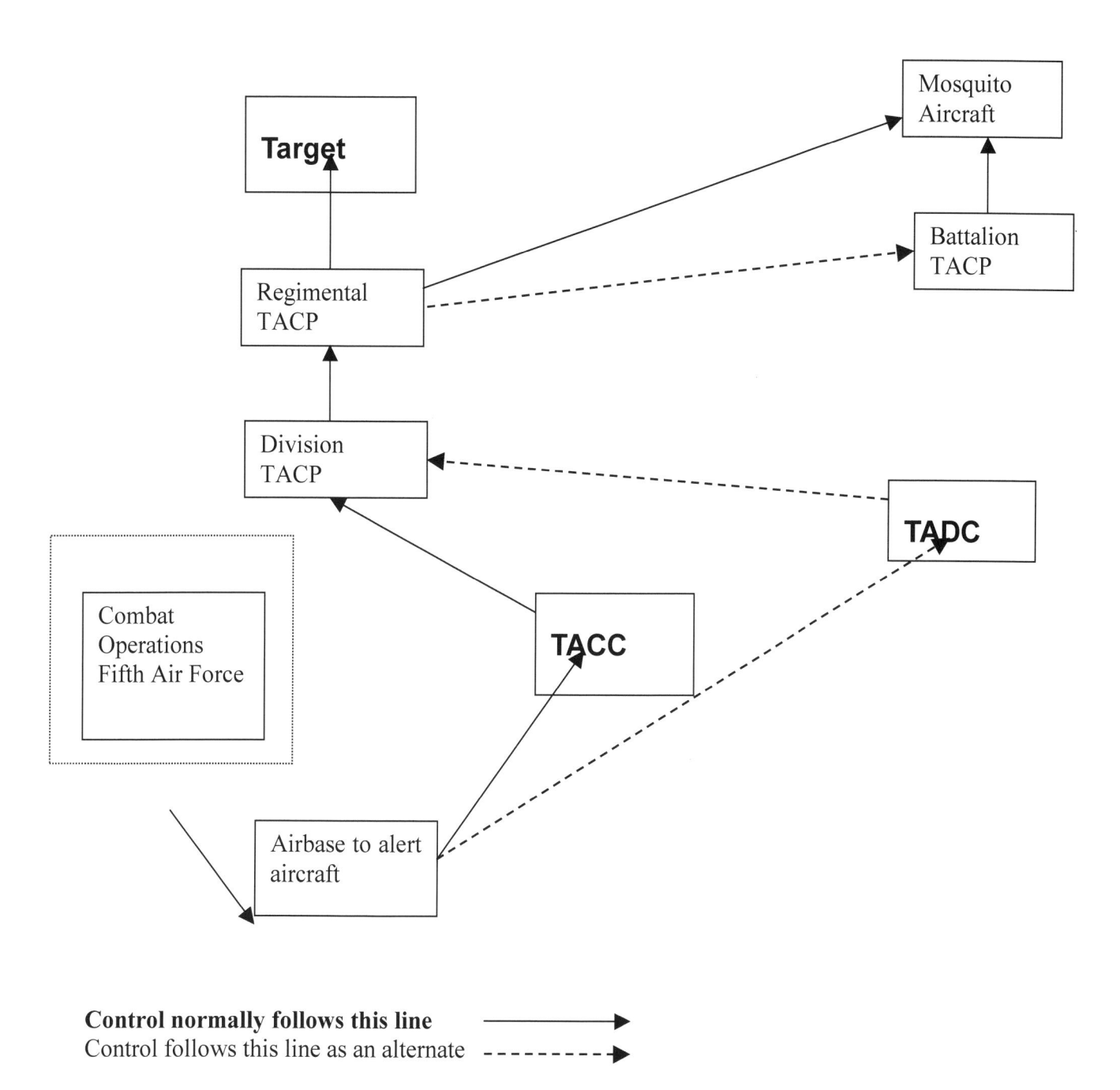

Control normally follows this line ⟶
Control follows this line as an alternate ╌╌╌⟶

Source: V.E. MeGee, "Tactical Air Support of Ground Forces," *Marine Corps Gazette*, December 1955, 15.

Figure 9. Army-Air Force Execution Procedure Korea

The FEC was a unified command on paper; in practice, it was an Army organization. Staffed mostly with Army personnel the FEC did not establish a joint staff Policy or joint forces beyond an amphibious task force.[193] General MacArthur established a non-doctrinal means to exercise command and delegated his authority for air operations in Korea to the FEAF, commanded by Lieutenant General George Stratemeyer. On 8 July 1950, MacArthur issued a theater policy directive establishing "coordination control."[194] He failed to publish any accompanying explanation of the term, associated procedures, or command responsibilities. The use of a non-standard doctrinal term confused both air and ground commanders greatly. The omission of even a definition caused even greater confusion between the Air Force and the Navy. No one knew how "coordination control" was to work in practice, but everyone seemed to have an interpretation of its meaning.[195] The Sterns Mission reported that communication between services and units resulted in a failure to coordinate operations, caused disagreements over the wording of important orders, and that this concept adversely affected tactical effectiveness of the FEAF.[196] Words do have meaning, and it was incumbent upon the FEC and FEAF to explain the meaning of coordination control in order to ensure understanding and to avoid failure based on miscommunication

General Stratemeyer wrote several memorandums to General MacArthur in the weeks before the latter's staff issued the theater directive on "coordination control." Stratemeyer asked MacArthur for operational control of all land-based naval aviation when operating over North Korea or from Japan. Stratemeyer also requested the operational control of naval land-based aviation operating from South Korean bases.

---

[193] Department of the Air Force, "Korean Evaluation Project: Report on Air Operations" (Sterns Mission), 16 January 1951, 20 (ASHAF-A, K168.041-2).
[194] Dept. USAF, Sterns Mission, 20 (ASHAF-A, K168.041-2). (The Sterns mission sights 13 July as the date of the theater directive on Coordination Control from the FEC. However, the Barcus Mission explains the origin and timeline of its development and implementation starting with the 8 July 1950 letter from GHQFEC, MGen Almond on Coordination of the Air Effort).
[195] Dept. USAF, Sterns Mission, 20 (ASHAF-A, K168.041-2).
[196] Ibid.

He expressed the desire to place these air units under the authority of Fifth Air Force.[197] It appears that his desire was to place air control of Korea under the direct authority of one air asset manager, which reflected the doctrine written in FM 31-35 and FM 100-20. Stratemeyer wrote,

> In the case of the carrier-based aviation in order that proper coordination can be maintained with my bomber command (B-29's) and the Fifth Air Force. I must be able to direct their operations including the targets to be hit and the area in which they must operate.[198]

Over the next several weeks, General Stratemeyer worked to establish the FEAF as the single air manager in Korea. He exchanged numerous letters and memorandums with GHQFEC, writing to General MacArthur, while the Chief of Staff, GHQFEC, Major General Almond provided, the responses to the FEAF request. Major General Almond sent a joint letter to the CG, FEAF, and Commander of USNF-FE delegating operational controlling authority of air assets. Almond issued MacArthur's order, assigning operational control over all aircraft operating in the execution of the FEAF mission. He also assigned operational control of all aircraft in execution of the USNF-FE over water.[199]

Almond's letter complicated the command relationship and controlling responsibilities by giving authority to control naval aircraft when not in support of the Navy's mission to the FEAF. The naval air missions cited in the letter included naval reconnaissance, anti-submarine warfare, and support of naval tasks such as amphibious

---

[197] Lieutenant General G.E. Stratemeyer, Commanding General, FEAF, memorandum to Douglas MacArthur, General of the Army, subject: Naval Units, 8 July 1950 (ASHAF-A, *An Evaluation of the Effectiveness of the United States Air Force in the Korean Campaign*, Barcus Report Command Relationships, Appendix 2 Book II, Documentation to the Operations Narrative, K168.041-1, v-9).

[198] Stratemeyer, memorandum, 8 July 1950 (ASHAF-A, K168.041-1, v-9).

[199] Major General Edward M. Almond, Joint letter to Commanding General, FEAF and to Commander, USNF-FE, subject: Coordination of Air Effort of Far East Air Forces and United States Naval Forces, Far East, 8 July 1950 (ASHAF-A, *An Evaluation of the Effectiveness of the United States Air Force in the Korean Campaign*, Barcus Report Command Relationships, Appendix 2 Book II, Documentation to the Operations Narrative, K168.041-1, v-9).

assault.[200] These two letters seemed to create an atmosphere that should have stimulated a close working relationship by creating areas and sectors of responsibility for each command. Major General Almond's letter implied that, under normal operating procedures, the Navy authority extended to control of air over water and the FEAF authority extended over the land. However, it is easy to see that in practice this arrangement of command and operational control of air assets would create confusion and conflict. The FEAF questioned naval authority to conduct air interdiction operations over North Korea in support of naval objectives. The failure to establish detailed coordination with the Navy resulted in confusion at the major supporting command level in part because no one understood the meaning of "coordination control" or its implied tasks for subordinate commanders.

Almond's directive sought to maintain overall command and control of all air assets at the GHQFEC level. GHQFEC retained basic selection and priority of target areas under its target analysis group. The GHQFEC would continue to assign tasks and prescribe coordination by delegation of specific areas of operation, while it delegated "coordination control" to the FEAF.[201] A staff officer at GHQFEC offered one interpretation of "coordination control":

> Coordination control is the authority to prescribe methods and procedures to effect coordination in the operation of air elements of two or more forces operating in the same area. It comprises the authority to disapprove operations of one force which might interfere with the operations of another force and to coordinate air efforts of the major FEC commands by such means as prescribing boundaries between operating areas, time of operations in areas, and measures of identification between air elements.[202]

The concept of "coordination control" in this contexts seems very similar to the present concept of the airspace control authority under the current JFACC doctrine. Under closer inspection the "coordination control" directive implied that the CINCFE desired to retain command and some control of air operations as he was able, rather than issuing total responsibility to subordinate echelons. It is likely that General Almond

---

[200] Almond, letter 8 July 1950 (ASHAF-A, K168.041-1, v-9).
[201] Almond, letter 8 July 1950 (ASHAF-A, K168.041-1, v-9).
[202] Command and Organization, vol.1, book I, 14 (Barcus Mission, ASHAF-A, K168.041-1, v-1).

and other staff members of FEC kept unity of command as an overriding principle component of the GHQ war fighting philosophy. General Mark Clark stated in several letters to the Chief of Staff of the Army that the ground commander must exercise operational control of tactical air assets to ensure unity of command over the battlefield.[203]

General Clark later became CINCFEC in May 1952 when he replaced General Ridgeway. General Almond, as Commander of Tenth Corps, expressed his opinion on numerous occasions, stating that the ground commander must have operational control of tactical air assets to ensure proper utilization and unity of command.[204] He often cited the Navy-Marine system of CAS as a useful model. Almond advocated a tactical air support structure that provided unity of command under the ground commander and flexibility in tactical air support planning and control.[205] He advocated the decentralization of tactical air support down to the battalion level to break down an Air Force system he saw as unresponsive to the ground commander.[206] The Marine system used a centralized tactical air command structure oriented on providing responsive flexible support to the ground mission generally ahead of other mission tasks.

The problem with an attached and dedicated tactical air support process is that there is a finite amount of air available to commit to the war effort at any given time. To assign aircraft as an organic asset to the battalion would undercut the flexibility of aviation to respond to unexpected battlefield events. It is difficult at times for ground commanders to project and determine air targets more than twelve to twenty-four hours in advance. If the enemy moves or does not cooperate with the ground commander's

---

[203] General Mark Clark, Office, Chief of US Army Field Forces, to Chief of Staff of the Army, subject: Tactical Air Support for Ground Forces, 13 September 1951. and General Mark Clark, Office, Chief of US Army Field Forces, to Chief of Staff of the Army, subject: Army Requirements for Close Tactical Air Support, 24 October 1950y TacAir Memorandum, Tactical Air Support for Ground Forces Memo, 13 September 1951, http://carlisle-www.army.mil/cgi-bin/usamhi/DL/).
[204] Michael Lewis, "Lieutenant General, Ned Almond, USA: A Ground Commanders Conflicting view with Airmen over CAS Doctrine and Employment," (SAAS thesis, Air University, June 1996), 91-95.
[205] Lewis, 94.
[206] Lewis, 93.

plan, these sorties might be better used elsewhere. The opposite is also true in that the lack of attention to close support targets could allow a breakthrough or an offensive to continue to roll forward. Targeting the enemy is key to successful operation in the air and on the ground and it is not an easy task with an uncooperative and thinking enemy.

There are two competing methods of reaching the same war-winning objectives, which the "coordination control" debate brought out. The Air Force, using FM 31-35, fought tooth and nail to optimize air assets under a single asset manager. The Air Force vision was to assign assets to targets based on strategic and theater priorities. In essence, the Air Force was attempting to practice a "just-in-time" method of CAS at the tactical level. The FEAF air plan in Korea was to provide just enough CAS to plug the holes as they appeared in the ground battle, but to concentrate on the attrition of Communist war-fighting capability through strategic and air interdiction missions. The Air Force viewed airpower as a combat arm separate and distinct from other forces in capability.

The Army saw as its task stepping toe-to-toe with the Communist and bloody them with superior firepower, tactics, and operational maneuver. The Army wanted to practice a method of war-fighting that would optimize its traditional ground force efforts. By having organic weapons used in conjunction with artillery and CAS the Army could concentrate on the attrition of the Communist in the close battle while still conducting the deep battle on a lower priority. The Army owned artillery and organic direct fire weapons, however it did not own a tactical air force. The Army saw air support as another weapon in the arsenal, but the Army had to ask other services with different priorities to support their air support requests. The lack of a delineated command relationship and responsibility gave the Army an opportunity to ask the Navy for CAS assets in support of Army objectives. The Army made these requests soon after the establishment of "coordination control" without the FEAF's knowledge, creating confusion, potential flight hazards, and degrading the efficiency of tactical air assets.

The connectivity and coordination of air operations between Fifth Air Force, Eighth Army, and Seventh Fleet was spotty at best during the first four months of the war. FEAF coordination with Eighth Army in Korea was disjointed and incomplete. The

Sterns and Barcus Missions reported that inadequate communication and coordination had led to impotent joint action and the underutilization of air assets.[207] This fact was demonstrated during July 1950, when aircraft from Combined Task Force (CTF) 77 flew ground support mission in support of Eighth Army requests at the same time these mission requests were being filled by Fifth Air Force.[208] Confusion reigned because no one knew the command relationship created by "coordination control." Yet everyone assumed an understanding of the term and that created faulty command relationships. The FEAF saw itself as the senior air command but complicated the issue by delegating "coordination control" to Fifth Air Force to act as the only air manager for Eighth Army. Eighth Army did not agree with this interpretation of "coordination control" and requested air support direct from Seventh Fleet.[209] The separate tasking of air by Eighth Army created all kinds of air space control issues in the theater both for the Navy and Fifth Air Force, concerning safety of flight and the most effective use of air assets.

The questions surrounding "coordination control" remained through the war for FEAF, USNF-FE, and the Marines. The FEAF, USNF-FE, Eighth Army, and the Marines worked out the command relationships as necessary to conduct an effective campaign in Korea, but the process was slow. Initially, the process of coordination took place only at the highest policymaking levels of command in Tokyo. The three major services' theater headquarters (GHQFEC, FEAF, and USNF-FE) initiated the coordination process using personal contacts. They also used staff briefings attended by command and staff personnel of all three services, communication between Joint Strategic Plans and Operations Group (JSPOG) and the service component theater headquarters to ensure everyone understood the situation. The top-level policy staffs sent out liaison officers to aid in the coordination process.[210] The failure to develop

---

[207] Dept. USAF, Sterns Mission, 23 (ASHAF-A, Maxwell AFB, Ala 36112, K168.041-2, 25 June-December 1950) and Department of the Air Force, *An Evaluation of the United States Air Force in the Korean Campaign*, Command and Organization, vol.1, book I, 14 (Barcus Mission, ASHAF-A, K168.041-1, v-1).
[208] Department of the Air Force, *An Evaluation of the United States Air Force in the Korean Campaign*, Command And Organization, vol.1, book I, 17 (Barcus Mission, ASHAF-A, K168.041-1, v-1).
[209] Ibid., 17-18. (Barcus Mission, ASHAF-A, K168.041-1, v-1).
[210] Ibid., 75-76. (Barcus Mission, ASHAF-A, K168.041-1, v-1).

clear command relationships and responsibilities may have had a greater adverse impact on the first month and a half of the war than any other factor. During August and September of 1950, the services developed command relationships, workable processes, and solidified service responsibilities.[211]

The Marines were very concerned about the organizational structure of theater air command and control. The 1st MAW's squadron locations ranged across the FEC's area of responsibility. The Marines based aircraft in Japan, on US Navy escort carriers off the coast of Korea, and on US air bases in Korea. They were especially concerned about how Marine aviation assets would fit into the Korean theater air command organization. Major General Craig sought General MacArthur's approval for the Marines to fight as they trained in August 1950.[212] MacArthur approved the request. As the war progressed, the FEAF increasingly directed Marine tactical air support to shift its effort away from Marine units and the Marine control system to support other UN units and the Air Force system of control. Marine tactical air units were able to support other UN forces as well as the Marine ground units due to the maintenance of air supremacy, and the large numbers of aircraft available in theater.[213]

Except for formally checking in with Fifth Air Force Tactical Air Control Center (TACC) and the JOC, Marine aviation, when operated in support of Marine ground units, operated in accordance with Navy-Marine Corps doctrine.[214] When they operated in support of UN units the Marines operated in accordance with the Army-Air Force control system.[215]

From August through September 1950, Marine air support focused its effort on supporting the Marines on the Pusan Perimeter.[216] In late September through December

---

[211] Ibid., 72. (Barcus Mission, ASHAF-A, K168.041-1, v-1).
[212] Major General Edward A. Craig, 41. (Historical Division, Headquarters, U.S. Marine Corps, The Pusan Perimeter through Pohang Commitment, CD-ROM collection of Korean War Historical Documents, CD No.14 of 24).
[213] The Korean War Project, "An Evaluation of the Influence of the Marine Corps," Section IV-B-9 (MCUA Box 1, folder 27).
[214] Ibid., Section IV-B-9 (MCUA Box 1, folder 27).
[215] Ibid., Section IV-B-10 (MCUA Box 1, folder 27).
[216] C.B. Cates, Commandant of the Marine Corps (CMC), memorandum to Chief of Naval Operations (CNO), subject: Employment of 1st MAW in Support of 1st Marine Division in Korea, 31 May 1951 (Korean War Project at MCUA Box 14, folder 15).

1950, the Marine aviators supported Seventh Infantry Division and Tenth Corps during the Inchon to Seoul Operations. USNF-FE exercised control over the amphibious objective area in accordance with Navy-Marine Corps doctrine.[217] Again, in January 1951, Marine aviation received direction from FEAF to shifted its fighting effort away from supporting Marine ground units. The FEAF directed Marine air to support Fifth Air Force interdiction and armed reconnaissance first, and to provide CAS on an as available basis irrespective of service doctrine and request.[218]

The FEAF obtained from GHQFEC control of all aviation over Korea including Navy flights over land in July 1950. The GHQFEC action placed all tactical air forces operating in Korea under the FEAF as a single air manager. The FEAF designated Fifth Air Force as its controlling authority in Korea.[219] Fifth Air Force officially assigned 1st MAW to operate in direct supporting of Tenth Corps during operations in Northeast Korea.[220] During the later phases of the Korean War, Fifth Air Force directed all aircraft in Korea to missions by "fire hose effect," assigning missions to aircraft on an "as available" basis and ensuring a large volume of missions supported CAS operations.[221]

General Clifton B. Cates, the Commandant of the Marine Corps (CMC), working through the Chief of Naval Operations (CNO), attempted to influence the organizational structure and employment of Marine aviation in Korea. By May 1951, it had changed

---

[217] C.B. Cates, 31 May 1951 (Attachment draft memorandum prepared by CMC for the CNO for the Joint Chiefs of Staff, this three page memorandum addresses the Marine Corps concerns with regard to the manner of employment of the 1st MAW in Korea since January 1951), 2. (The Korean War Project, Close Air Support of 1st Marine Division: Letters and Extracts Supporting CMC Representation to JCS through CNO (this memorandum is part of the Korean War Project at MCUA Box 14, folder 15).
[218] Ibid., 1.
[219] Lieutenant General George E. Stratemeyer, Commanding General, Far East Air Forces, Letter to General of the Army, Douglas MacArthur, subject: Close Support for Ground Troops in Korea, 17 July 1950 (Barcus Mission, ASHAF-A, K168.041-1, v-1, appendix 2, book II).
[220] The Korean War Project, "An Evaluation of the Influence of the Marine Corps," Section IV-B-19 (MCUA Box 1, folder 27).
[221] Department of the Air Force, *An Evaluation of the United States Air Force in the Korean Campaign, Operations and Tactics*, vol. III, 17 (Barcus Mission, ASHAF-A, K168.041-1, v-3).

significantly from the early days of August 1950 when the Marine Corps first went ashore in Korea. Cates, writing to the CNO, stated,

> Reports reaching me…on this matter have confirmed my view regarding the steady deterioration of air support received by the 1st Marine Division in Korea. This has reached such a state that I consider it a matter of the utmost seriousness. My information indicates that the system of air support employed by Navy and Marine units from August through December with spectacularly successful results as even the Army admitted, no longer exists in Korea. In its place, a vastly different method is being employed. It would appear that this method being arbitrarily imposed, largely for the sake of uniformity alone, on units capable of far higher standards. In my opinion, if this situation is allowed to go unchallenged, the proven superiority of the Navy-Marine Corps system, even for our own purposes, will eventually be discredited. In such circumstances the loss to the national defense in general and the naval service in particular will be great.[222]

The CAS system used in amphibious operations is not materially different from the air support furnished for normal ground operations. The principles and functions are generally the same for both operations. Most of the techniques, terminology, and communications nets are also similar.[223]

The differences between the Navy-Marine System and the Air Force system were seemingly minor, but during operations in Korea the Navy-Marine system proved most effective in air-ground operations. A Marine division maintains 13 TACPs permanently assigned as an organic part of the division, whereas a fixed number of such teams were not always provided to an Army division.

In amphibious operations, the tactical air direction center (TADC) normally assigned aircraft to carry out air request missions, whereas in normal air-ground operations this function is retained at the next higher echelon, the tactical air control center (TACC).

Requests for support missions, reconnaissance and supply, as well as air support, were forwarded to the TADC over existing air support communication nets and

---

[222] C.B. Cates, 31 May 1951 (The Korean War Project, Close Air Support of 1st Marine Division: Letters and Extracts Supporting CMC Representation to JCS through CNO, This memorandum is part of the Korean War Project at MCUA Box 14, folder 15).
[223] Lieutenant Colonel Allan G. Pixton, "Close Air Support in Amphibious Operations," *Military Review* (August 19530), 27-34.

channels. The Army and the Air Force communicated requests from subordinate units to the JOC. Pre-planned and supply missions used a separate communication system to make requests. Under the Navy and Marine system, requests for tactical air support passed directly from the TACP to the TADC, which resulted in speedier and arguably more efficient support for ground units.

The Army-Air Force assigned TACPs to the regimental level. CAS responsiveness and effectiveness might have increased had TACPs been assigned to the battalion level on a permanent basis. The other requirement necessary to ensure readiness and success was proper training and coordination. The FEAF and Eighth Army did not train and coordinate prior to the start of the Korean War. During the early stages of amphibious landings, the landing force is completely dependent on air support and Naval gunfire. Important to the effectiveness of these fires is timeliness, accuracy, and a volume sufficient to influence the battle in the amphibious objective area (AOA).

The organizational structure and command relationships of service component headquarters had an immediate impact on the tactical air support mission. The use of non-standard terms adversely affected the Korean tactical air organization and created confusion and disputes between the principle commands. The best way to prepare for and execute tactical air operations in an air campaign is to train to an agreed upon standard.

Commanders at all levels are obligated to structure tactical air operations in accordance with the established standard and processes when conflicts first arise and then react to the changing situation. During the first four months of the war, many came to realize there was a doctrinal plan in place for fighting a tactical air war. The organization and understanding of established Army-Air Force processes for employment of tactical air support by top-level Army and Air Force commanders was sound and focused. The subordinate Army-Air Force command echelons seemed to have a very different organizational understanding of the same processes in practice. The segmented service component structure and lack of joint training before and during the first year of the war created a problem of coordination. The Army and the Air Force were reluctant to man the command and control system structure down to the TACP level due to personnel limitations, which compounded coordination problems and directly affected the means of control.

The Means and Effectiveness of Command and Control (C2):

Because of the employment of tactical air support during the Korean War it is evident that there is a direct correlation between the means of C_2 and its effectiveness. Both the Army-Air Force and the Navy-Marine systems of C_2 employed in the Korean theater of operations claimed to be effective in achieving desired objectives. In practice, the Navy-Marine C_2 received better press with regard to its support to ground troops.

The Navy-Marine system manned its TACPs to the battalion level front-line units. Before the Inchon landing, in preparation for operations in northeast Korea, the Marines added one pilot forward air controller (FAC) to the TACP team.[224] The Marines perceived the advantage to be more dynamic control with the added controller. One FAC could move forward to observe targets while the other FAC could provide advice to the battalion commander on air issues and coordinate air support with other supporting arms.[225]

The Army-Air Force system of C_2 manned TACPs randomly to the regimental headquarters level. These TACPs were not normally in sight of the frontlines resulting in their being employed more like a TADC trying to execute as a FAC. Eighth Army received the preponderance of TACP teams, while Tenth Corps TACP manning was hit or miss.[226]

The Air Force relied on the Mosquito, airborne tactical air controllers (TAC (A)), to control forward at the frontline and beyond the bomb safety line.[227] There was a problem, however, with both the Air Force TACP and the Mosquito controllers. The Mosquito observers and the TACP controllers normally only served a short tour. The

---

[224] The Korean War Project, "An Evaluation of the Influence of the Marine Corps," vol. 1, Section IV-B-21 (MCUA Box 1, folder 27).
[225] Ibid.
[226] Department of the United States Air Force, *An Evaluation of the United States Air Force in the Korean Campaign*, Barcus Mission, Air-Ground Team, vol. II, 19 (ASHAF-A, K168.041-2).

Mosquito ground force observer served a short period and then returned to his ground job.[228] Usually these ground observers sent to the Mosquitoes went for rest.[229] The alertness, interest, and efficiency of these observers in light of this fact then become suspect.

The Marines used Mosquito control and employed organic observation aircraft, the OY-2, to spot and adjust artillery fires and to control air strikes. The FAC used the OY to direct air when he could not expose himself to enemy fire. Major Vincent J. Gottschalk, commander VMO-6, reported that the OY, like the Mosquito, was able to locate targets from the air and that they operated in conjunction with the ground FAC coordinating CAS missions in support of ground troops. The Marine TACP monitored the missions and cancelled them if the OY was in error or if the situation had changed.[230] Under the Air Force control system, this safety feature of having a ground FAC available to cancel the attack run was not normally available at this level of control.

There was a tendency to minimize the importance of the TACP by the Air Force. The TACP lacked the necessary attention it required to perform its function.[231] The marginalized TACP resulted in an organization that lacked composition, equipment, and written procedures on how to conduct a CAS mission.[232] The TACP controllers served a three-week tour of duty.[233]

---

[227] The Korean War Project, "An Evaluation of the Influence of the Marine Corps," vol. 1, Section IV-B-21 (MCUA Box 1, folder 27).
[228] Department of the United States Air Force, *An Evaluation of the United States Air Force in the Korean Campaign*, Barcus Mission, Air-Ground Team, vol. II, 22 (ASHAF-A, K168.041-2).
[229] Ibid.
[230] Major Vincent J. Gottschalk, Commander, VMO-6, 1st MAW, transcript, interviewed by Captain S.W. Higginbotham, 31 March 1951 (USMCHD, The Pusan Perimeter through Pohang Commitment, CD-ROM collection of Korean War Historical Documents, CD No.14 of 24).
[231] Department of the United States Air Force, *Summary of An Evaluation of the United States Air Force in the Korean Campaign*, Barcus Mission, Air-Ground Team, vol. II thru VII, 14 (ASHAF-A, K168.041-2).
[232] Barcus Mission, Air-Ground Team, vol. II, 19 (ASHAF-A, K168.041-2, 25 June-December 1950).
[233] Ibid., vol. II, 18 (ASHAF-A, K168.041-2).

The short tours for both of these critical positions certainly resulted in a low development of expertise and ability. Army and Air Force controllers left their assignments just as they had reached a minimum level of proficiency. Some Air Force pilots viewed TACP duty as distasteful and felt that even three weeks was too long a tour, while other pilots advocated a longer tour.[234] The Marine Corps directed Marine pilots to TACP duty. It is certain that some pilots found the duty not to their liking, but even these pilots knew the tour was for the good of the Corps and they did want to fly again. Most Marine TACP tours lasted about six months and in some cases up to a year.[235]

In addition to the short tours there were no standard CAS control procedures issued and coordinated within the air-ground organizations of the Army and the Air Force.[236] Controllers, observers, and pilots lacked the requisite training before their assignment to TACP duty. They attempted to improvise and establish workable procedures among individuals and units by coordinating with artillery officers, but the close control procedures varied greatly between divisions.[237] Marine pilots assigned to battalions before the war trained for the TACP mission on a regular basis. The Marine Air Control Groups (MACG) conducted a FAC training program established to educate and qualify FACs in the C_2 system and its procedures. The course of study was extensive and included the Navy-Marine C_2 system and control procedures, as well as the Army-Air Force system.[238]

The Air Force C_2 system equipment and communication devices needed improvement early in the war but with attention and time, the Air Force corrected these

---

[234] Ibid., vol. II, 18 (ASHAF-A, K168.041-2).
[235] Captain James D. Boldman, transcript of oral interview by S.W. Higginbotham, 1st Provisional Historical Platoon, 24 January 1951 (USMCHD, The Pusan Perimeter through Pohang Commitment, CD-ROM collection of Korean War Historical Documents, CD No.14 of 24).
[236] Barcus Mission, Air-Ground Team, vol. II, 19 (ASHAF-A, K168.041-2).
[237] Ibid.
[238] *Manual for Forward Air Control*, Marine Air Control Group 2, 26 August 1952 (MCUA, KW Project, Box 16, Folder 11).

problems.[239] The real problems remained poor communication and coordination between the front and the JOC. The lack of TACPs and qualified controllers on the frontlines compounded the problem and created an even greater lapse in response time for CAS missions to divert from interdiction and arrive at the proper regimental location ready for a CAS mission. The lack of close coordination between commands and organizations across service boundaries compromised the effectiveness of the Army-Air Force control system.

The method of CAS control exercised by the Marine Corps owed its success in large part to its complete ground communication systems. The teamwork of the Marine Air Wing and the Marine division improved the reliability of the communication system. Joint training in peacetime re-enforced the principles of teamwork and system familiarization provided an opportunity to evaluate and teach doctrine.[240]

The JOC normally assigned greater than fifty per cent of Marine aviation's daily missions as scheduled pre-planned missions based on the previous day's estimate.[241] The impact was that it limited flexibility and placed air at a disadvantage based on time to respond to immediate targets that develop during the course of the battle. Prior to launch the control system gambled that known targets would not move and that the fragile control and communication systems would work at 100% efficiency in order to respond to request. A twenty-minute response time from notification to aircraft overhead was a reasonable goal.

Before the summer of 1951, Marine tactical air in Korea operated in direct support of Tenth Corps and used the Navy-Marine air-ground system. Aircraft were available on alert to respond to requests from the front. The Marine Tactical Air Control Center (MTACC) maintained launch authority over aircraft. TACPs could request air directly

---

[239] Dept. of the Air Force, *Summary of An Evaluation of the United States Air Force in the Korean Campaign*, Operations and Tactics, book II, vol. I, 14 (Barcus Mission, ASHAF-A, K168.041-1, v-1).
[240] The Korean War Project, "An Evaluation of the Influence of the Marine Corps", vol. 1, Section III-C-2 (MCUA Box 1, folder 27).
[241] Major Wade W. Larkin, Commanding Officer, Marine Tactical Air Control Squadron (MTACS) 2, transcript of oral interview by Captain Nolan J. Beat, 29 June 1951 (USMCHD, The Pusan Perimeter through Pohang Commitment, CD-ROM collection of Korean War Historical Documents, CD No.14 of 24).

from the MTACC. Other agencies monitored the tactical air request (TAR) net along the chain of command, remaining silent unless they intended to deny the request. Aircraft availability under this system was high. The system responded within minutes generally.[242]

By the summer of 1951, the control system changed due to the reorganization of command relationships. Eighth Army assumed control of Tenth Corps and the 1st Marine Division. Marine aviation used the Army-Air Force air-ground system. Requests for air support required authorization for a phone patch to Eighth Army. The Marine senior controller contacted an Eighth Army watch officer within the JOC via the chain of command, via the approved phone patch. The controller then passes the target and controller information to the Army watch officer. The Army watch officer discussed the request with the Air Force watch officer. If approved, the watch officer forwards the request to the JOC TACC. The JOC TACC diverts the next available armed reconnaissance mission reporting on station to "service" the immediate request. Response times under the Army-Air Force system averaged approximately an hour to an hour-and-a-half after the FAC passed his request to the Marine Air Support Section.[243]

The Marines considered the TACP and the associated equipment and connective processes of coordination a necessity to successful employment of CAS. The Army came to understand and appreciate the TACP as a critical element of the air-ground system. The Marines as well found added value in having a controller airborne to observe targets, fires, and events that were not visible from a ground location.

The Barcus mission reported that early in the war,

> The absence of a complete and properly functioning air-ground operations system left Headquarters, Eighth Army and Headquarters, Tenth Corps (Independent), in the position of not knowing accurately the close support needs of their combat units and of not having the means, in any event, to communicate these needs to Fifth Air Force in a prompt and acceptable

---

[242] Major Elton Meuller, Operations Officer, Marine Tactical Air Control Squadron (MTACS) 2, transcript of oral interview by Captain Nolan J. Beat, 13 December 1950 (USMCHD, The Pusan Perimeter through Pohang Commitment, CD-ROM collection of Korean War Historical Documents, CD No.14 of 24).

[243] Larkin, MTACS-2, transcript of oral interview by Captain Nolan J. Beat, 29 June 1951 (USMCHD, CD No.14 of 24).

manner.[244]

During the Inchon to Seoul operation, the Marines provided Tenth Corps and Seventh Infantry Division with CAS. The Marines, in preparation for the operation, provided three Marine TACPs to Tenth Corps and trained additional Army TACPs by mobile training teams to instruct the Seventh Infantry Division in the Navy-Marine method of CAS. Major General Almond believed that this action contributed to the uniformity of the air-ground system within Tenth Corps. He said the effective CAS provided by the Marines through the FACs with the Seventh Infantry Division greatly aided in the success of the Tenth Corps. Almond conducted a supporting arms exercise employing Seventh Infantry Division and 1st Marine Division with elements of 1st MAW aviation to demonstrate the effectiveness of close tactical air support.[245] Follow on operations into northeast Korea subsequently added to the belief that the Marines had a superior method of employing CAS.

Had the Seventh Infantry Division not received Marine support, the controversy that followed Inchon may not have had an impact on the Air Force as great as it did. The shortfalls of the Air Force system would not have seemed so great to those units and commanders involved. The politicians and the public may not have even known there was a controversy. The only indication at the start of the war was the Air Force and UN force failure to stop the North Koreans before Pusan.

From July 1950 through January 1951 there developed an air controversy that surrounded the CAS mission and the means of employing CAS assets in Korea. The Army perceived a difference between the Air Force and the Marine Corps's desire, determination, and capability to provide adequate tactical air support to ground units fighting in Korea. The air controversy developed in part due to complaints made by General Almond concerning the support he had received from Fifth Air Force when compared to Marine CAS. Lieutenant General Walker, however, expressed his pleasure

---

[244] Summary of An Evaluation of the United States Air Force in the Korean Campaign, book II, vol. I, 9 (Barcus Mission, ASHAF-A, K168.041-1, v-1).
[245] The Korean War Project, "An Evaluation of the Influence of the Marine," vol. 1, Section IV-B-15 (MCUA Box 1, folder 27).

with CAS provided by Fifth Air Force: "If it had not been for the air support that we received from the Fifth Air Force, we would not have been able to stay in Korea."[246]

The reach of Lieutenant General Walker's remarks and those of Major General Almond, along with the variations in the two C_2 systems, became the subject of heated debate in Washington, D.C. The controversy gained momentum after the UN forces were unable to slow the Communist advance south through Korea to Pusan. Congressman Carl Vinson, chairman of the House Armed Services Committee opened inquiries concerning Air Force efforts to provide adequate CAS to the Army.[247] Carl Vinson's investigation into tactical air operations in Korea led the Air Force to react to public allegations and to initiate a public relations campaign. The Air Force commissioned two investigations to evaluate Air Force effectiveness during the Korean War.[248] Mr. James A. McCone, Assistant Secretary of the Air Force, told Mr. Vinson that the Air Force intended to look into allegations that the Air Force was concentrating too much on strategic bombing and had forgotten the man with the rifle on the ground.[249]

The Air Force, under the principles of the doctrine in FM 31-35, believed in its cause, but it still feared for its existence, suspecting the Army of trying to reassume control and jurisdiction over the new service. General Almond's comments concerning

---

[246] Operations and Tactics, vol. III, 15 (Barcus Mission, ASHAF-A, K168.041-1, v-3) (The Honorable Melvin Price of Illinois repeated this same quotation on the floor of the US House of Representatives on Saturday, October 20, 1950. Mr. Price was a member of the House Armed Services Committee and an USAF air power advocate. In his remarks, he chastises his colleagues in Congress for spreading false information about the actions of the Air Force in Korea from June to October 1950. House, "Decision in Korea Through Air Power", 82nd Congress, 1st Session, 1950, Appendix to the Congressional Record A6888).

[247] Carl Vinson, Chairman, House, Committee on Armed Services, to General Hoyt S. Vandenberg, USAF Chief of Staff, letter subject: Invitation to attend special subcommittee meetings, 2 August 1950 (Stearns Mission, ASHAF-A, K168.041-1, v-20).

[248] Mr. Finletter, Mr. McCone, General Twining, General McIntyre, General Smith, Professor Leach, Memorandum for the Record, subject: Summary of Conclusions Reached at meeting 10 January 1951 (Stearns Mission, ASHAF-A, K168.041-1, v-20).

[249] House, Committee on Armed Services, Vinson Special Subcommittee: Hearings extract, H. Res. 617, On Manpower, Tuesday, October 3, 1950 (Stearns Mission, ASHAF-A, K168.041-1, v-20).

the effectiveness of Air Force support and execution of the CAS mission hit home with top-level Air Force leaders. They secured positive comments concerning the Air Force support of ground troops from General Walker and General MacArthur.[250]

The Secretary of the Air Force, W. Stuart Symington, solicited a November 1947 document from General Eisenhower.[251] Eisenhower supported the concept of three separate forces yet integrated and complementary in roles and structure based on air, land, and sea.[252] He supported the concept of the air forces operating under a single command and that this organizational structure would provide maximum flexibility to execute both strategic and tactical missions.[253] The Air Force, General Eisenhower wrote, is a vital arm and a specialized service force. He confirmed the need for the Air Force to control tactical air and to provide a specialized system for coordination based on his experiences in Europe during World War II.[254]

The Air Force might have suspected a political attempt by the Army to deny the new force its independence, but it seemed apparent during the first six weeks of the war that the system of control might very well be broken. Chairman Vinson on numerous occasions concluded that the Marine system for CAS was superior to the Air Force system.

The Sterns and Barcus Missions assigned to evaluate the Air Forces CAS performance in Korea returned with preliminary findings that supported the Air Force doctrinal foundations. However, they suggested improvements in training and

---

[250] W. Burton Leach, Department of the Air Force, Office of the Secretary, memorandum open, subject: Status of "Korean Evaluation Project", 9 January 1951 (Stearns Mission, ASHAF-A, K168.041-1, v-20).

[251] Dwight D. Eisenhower, letter, subject: personal for W. Stuart Symington, The Secretary of the Air Force acknowledging a request for a secret memorandum dated 3 November 1947, March 8, 1950 (Stearns Mission, ASHAF-A, K168.041-1, v-20).

[252] Dwight D. Eisenhower, Chief of Staff of the Army, memorandum for the Secretary of Defense, subject: Tactical Air Support, 3 November 1947 (Stearns Mission, ASHAF-A, K168.041-1, v-20).

[253] Ibid.

[254] Ibid.

education of personnel, coordination with other services, joint operations and training, personnel changes, and TACP fixes to equipment and training.[255]

The Air Force concluded by November 1950 that the system was not completely broken but it did need some significant adjustments. The first item taken for action by the Air Force was to overcome the perceived quality shortfalls of the Air Force air-ground system by applying FEAF aircraft in larger numbers to the CAS missions.[256] For the Air Force gaining and maintaining air supremacy over the Korean peninsula from the start of the war ensured that quantity would not be a factor of criticism. At one point in the Korean campaign, the Air Force provided 70% of all FEAF aircraft for CAS. The total bomber effort devoted to CAS averaged 29.4%, as compared with 12.5% during World War II.[257] The Marines would argue that quality in CAS was better than quantity of sorties with no FAC direction. The Air Force might have agreed with the Marines on this point, but they were reacting to crises on a daily basis and quantity was a quick and easy answer when the Air Force needed time to fix other deficiencies.

The next task undertaken was to send liaison officers to the major supported commands. The Air Force leadership established coordination efforts at the top-level early in the war and initiated an education and public policy program to teach anyone who would listen, and especially their own airmen, about Air Force doctrine and philosophy.[258] By the end of 1951, the Air Force had gained greater command of it coordination and control problems and had successfully installed its version of an air-ground system over the Navy-Marine system.[259]

Three actions enabled the Air Force to gain greater influence over tactical air operations. Eighth Army assumed operational control of Tenth Corps and the corps no

---

[255] Leach, Status of "Korean Evaluation Project," 9 January 1951 (Stearns Mission, ASHAF-A, K168.041-1, v-20).
[256] Operations and Tactics, vol. III, 17 (Barcus Mission, ASHAF-A, K168.041-1, v-3).
[257] Ibid.
[258] Dept. USAF, *An Evaluation of the United States Air Force in the Korean Campaign*, Command And Organization, vol.1, book I, 72 (Barcus Mission, ASHAF-A, K168.041-1, v-1).
[259] Millet, *Semper Fidelis*, 502.

longer operated as an independent element.[260] The 1st Marine Division operated as part of Ninth Corp in April 1951, while 1st MAW operated as directed by the JOC.[261] This action kept the MAW from providing priority support to the 1st Marine Division.[262] The Fifth Air Force insisted that all air operations be coordinated through the JOC, which meant that 1st MAW would support all of Eighth Army. General Almond and General Shepard (Commanding General, Fleet Marine Forces Pacific) argued that the JOC neither focused on CAS nor was responsive enough to ground requirements.[263] By July 1951 changes in major commands quieted criticism of the Army-Air Force system.[264]

The Marines and the Navy resisted the Army-Air Force air-ground system doctrine until the end of the war.[265] The Marines were successful in wresting 1st MAW support from Fifth Air Force in May of 1952 as part of a training quota program, which Eighth Army interrupted as the Marines controlling their on air missions in direct support.[266] The General Barcus ended the practiced.[267] 1st MAW at the end of the war was supporting one out of every five Fifth Air Force CAS missions and came away convinced the Navy-Marine system the better of the two control systems.[268]

The argument presented by the Air Force to disregard the Marine system was that it was too costly in terms of manpower and air assets. A problem discussed by most advocates was what the term close support meant to each of the services. The Air Force seemed to interpret close as within the bomb line in the contact zone. The Marines determined close to be between 50 to 500 yards from friendly troops.

Marine General Silverthorn testifying before the House Armed Services Committee in September 1950, relayed a story of a young Marine Lieutenant:

> The Lieutenant participating and the battle for No-Name Ridge on the Natkong River-line described the close air support received.... The air support was so close that when the planes pulled out of their attack dives

---

[260] Ibid., 503.
[261] Ibid., 502.
[262] Millett, "Korea, 1950-1953," 378.
[263] Ibid.
[264] Ibid., 380
[265] Ibid., 387-390.
[266] Ibid., 390.
[267] Ibid.
[268] Ibid., 391.

the North Korean were within hand grenade distance.[269]

Similar to today's debate over the location of the Fire Support Coordination Line (FSCL), Air Force and Army/Marine leaders argued over the location of a coordination line. The Air Force argued in 1950 that the line was too far from friendly lines beyond the range of friendly artillery and that the line was arbitrarily drawn along a gridline rather than a terrain feature creating problems for aviators flying over the ground.

The Air Force, by not employing weapons to within 200 yards, may have unknowingly created a sanctuary for the enemy to hide in. The Chinese could easily conduct infiltration operations without UN forces knowledge and did on numerous occasions. The Chinese were able to accomplish this feat because of their lack of mechanization and limited lines of communication. The restrictive employment of air weapons close to troop was not overcome by the end of the war, both Generals Mark Clark and O.P. Weyland threaten to courts martial any pilot who dropped ordnance on friendly positions.[270] Fifth Air Force refused to change the air-ground control system and opted instead to brief in greater detail and to rely on positive Mosquito control.[271]

The Air Force applied airpower across the theater. The Air Force had difficulty finding interdiction targets after the first few months of the war and the Chinese would often retreat after an attack when they were making progress. It appeared that the Air Force was effective in its interdiction campaign. The Marines applied quality combat power close to friendly lines with great success. But the Marines left Korea unhappy with the method of the MAW's employment after June 1951. The task organization did not support Marine doctrine nor optimize its combat power as a force. It takes time for a strangulation strategy to become effective, and it is not responsive to immediate CAS requests. However, the Air Force continued to pursue the interdiction problem as its focus in Korea.

---

[269] Wade F. Fliesher, Colonel, USAF, Deputy Chief of Legislative Division, memorandum to General Hall, subject: Excerpts from Marine Corps Testimony on Tactical Aviation given to the House Armed Services Committee on 4 October 1950, 5 October 1950 (Stearns Mission, ASHAF-A, K168.041-1, v-20).
[270] Millett, "Korea, 1950-1953," 391.
[271] Ibid.

The Aircraft Basing Debate:

The basing of aircraft in the Korean War created a debate centered on access to the enemy targets, responsiveness, and sortie availability. The access to airfields and their proximity to the front lines influenced response time and sortie rates of tactical aircraft in Korea. It was a given that aviation needed bases from which to operate. Securing airfields on Korean soil, while maintaining carriers on the sea around the Korean peninsula, added to the flexibility of UN combat forces. The ground commander's CAS needs were based on simple requirements for air forces to provide responsive and effective CAS strikes.

The debate in Korea over basing pitted land-based aviation against carrier-based aviation and jets against propeller aircraft. Airfield distance from the front was a factor affecting CAS response time. It's a simple equation in terms of velocity multiplied by time equals distance. It was highly desirable to have your airfield as close behind you as possible. The Marines operated from bases both on the sea, in Korea, and from Japan. The CG, 1st MAW, thought airbases important enough to the success of the CAS mission to position aviation units forward in close proximity to forward units. The CG, 1st MAW, influenced the CG, Fifth Air Force, to move the Marine Wing from Kimpo to Wonsan, and then assigned them to Yonpo when Tenth Corps had secured Hamhung in Northeast Korea in an effort to provide responsive and effective CAS.[272] The Wing was in a good position then to support Tenth Corps and 1st Marine Division air requests when they arose.

The drawback to having air bases so close to the front is that those bases become vulnerable to attack by an adversary. When the Chinese pushed back the UN forces in northeast Korea during December 1950, the Chinese advance threatened US forward air bases. Fifth Air Force did its best to cover the withdrawal of Eighth Army in west Korea, but the disorderly retreat was harried and the Eighth Army left equipment on the field. The Marines in northeast Korea withdrew in order while maintaining an

---

[272] The Korean War Project, "An Evaluation of the Influence of the Marine Corps," vol. 1, Section IV-B-21 (MCUA Box 1, folder 27).

advanced base at Yonpo as a critical logistics link to the surrounded Marines.[273] Advanced air bases and air support played a critical role in the successful withdrawal.

The jet in Korea was a new air weapon, but was limited by its on-station time, only being able to stay up about half as long as the F-4U Corsair. But if an airfield was fifty miles from the front, a Korean War vintage jet could arrive at the front in about eight minutes; the F4U Corsair would take twenty-two minutes. But if the airfield was 150 miles away, the jet could stay on-station only about twenty-five minutes; the F4U could stay on-station for an hour and twenty minutes.[274] Most pilots saw the advantages of jet aviation over prop driven aircraft as speed and platform stability.[275] They anticipated technological advancements that would overcome the on-station time and ordnance limitations. Jets also required longer, harder, and clean runways as compared to prop aircraft.

Some pilots reported in interviews during the war that jet aircraft required far greater logistics and support then those required for propeller aircraft. During the period October 1951 through March 1952, an Air Force study looked at the aircraft maintenance workloads generated in Korean theater.[276] The study looked at battle damage, operational damage, ordinary maintenance, and modifications as the source for total maintenance man-hours expended by aircraft type and flight hour. The study evaluated the F-86, F-84, F-80, F-51, B-26, and B-29 across fourteen wings.[277] The study was inconclusive and sighted maintenance record keeping as a problem.[278] The

---

[273] Millett, Korea, 1950-1953, 372.
[274] Jack R. Cram and Col Charles L. Banks, "Win, Place, and Show for the Jets," *Marine Corps Gazette* (December 1951), 15.
[275] Captain Rodger Conant, VMF-311, transcript of oral interview by J.I. Kiernan, 23 January 1951 (USMCHD, The Pusan Perimeter through Pohang Commitment, CD-ROM collection of Korean War Historical Documents, CD No.14 of 24).
[276] Hugh J. Miser, *Operations Analysis Report no. 10: Aircraft Service Performance Evaluation Maintenance Workloads Generated in Korean Combat*, (Washington, D.C.: Operations Analysis Division, Director of Operations, Deputy Chief of Staff, Operations, Headquarters United States Air Force), i.
[277] Ibid., i, 9.
[278] Ibid., 5.

raw data seems to indicate that jet and prop aircraft required similar maintenance man-hours per combat flight hour generated.[279]

The additional fuel capacity at bases increased as well. Jets took 800 gallons of fuel or 32 drums to refuel. Marines at Yonpo refueled aircraft from drums by hand, which was easier to handle.[280] A squadron would need six, 3,200 gallon refueling tankers to support effective operations.[281] Prop driven aircraft, like the Corsair, could operate from unimproved airfields where jets had maintenance problems.[282]

The short deck of a carrier limited takeoff ordnance weight. The result was that carrier aviation, although more responsive, was less efficient per sortie than land based aircraft. Carrier air provided approximately 15% of the CAS missions while the land based aviation provided 85% of the sorties.[283] Additionally, the carriers retired to replenish food, ordnance, and fuel reserves. Carrier air made its first strikes into Korea on 3 July, but after eleven days the carrier went off-station.[284]

In the first two months of the Korean War, the Air Force, the Navy, and Marines all flew CAS missions from the carriers and escort carriers. Land-based aircraft operated from Korea and Japan, lengthening the recycle time of aircraft, while carriers could recycle aircraft quickly in comparison to Japan-based aircraft. The aircraft carrier could operate relatively close to the objective area and remain in the threat area for a short time. The carrier had one advantage over Korean land-based aircraft and that was in terms of the Korean environment. The aircraft operating from a carrier experienced less maintenance problems due to environmental conditions. The carrier protected the airplanes, the crews, and the maintenance areas from the Korean dust and weather.

---

[279] Ibid., 4.
[280] Major William E. Crowe, Operations Officer, VMF-311, transcript of oral interview by S.W. Higginbotham, 22 January 1951 (USMCHD, The Pusan Perimeter through Pohang Commitment, CD-ROM collection of Korean War Historical Documents, CD No.14 of 24).
[281] Crowe, transcript oral history, 22 January 1951.
[282] Captain William Magin, VMF-311, transcript of oral interview by S.W. Higginbotham, 23 January 1951 (USMCHD, The Pusan Perimeter through Pohang Commitment, CD-ROM collection of Korean War Historical Documents, CD No.14 of 24).
[283] Assistant Secretary of the Air Force, A Quantitative Comparison between Land-based and Carrier-based Air During the Korean War, June 1972, 7 (ASHAF-A, K143.61).

These general facts concerning aircraft carrier operations were as true in Korea as they were during World War II and today. The flexibility a carrier provided the FEC in Korea with attack options not available with an air force of only land-based assets.[285]

In June 1972, the Assistant Secretary of the Air Force conducted a quantitative comparison between land and sea based aviation during Korea, prepared by Directorate of General Purpose and Airlift Studies, Assistant Chief of Staff, Studies and Analysis, Headquarters, USAF. This report contains a brief history of the Korean War from 25 June through September 15 as a cross section of air application. The report focused on the period from the UN withdrawal from the 38th parallel to the Pusan perimeter and terminates just before the Inchon landing. It was limited in scope and lacked the necessary data to draw a distinct conclusion. The study failed to consider responsiveness, load, or flexibility. It provides a narrow look at this important issue from a decidedly pro-Air Force perspective. A key element not considered in the report and difficult to determine was the effect of CAS on enemy targets. The battle damage assessment (BDA) of each sortie was an elusive quantitative figure. A pilot may hit a target with his bomb load and score a battlefield kill, but in a few days or hours repairs are made or the target is moved, or stripped for parts. Proper and accurate BDA was a challenging art and scoring the effectiveness of CAS was as difficult in Korea as it is today.

The operational analysis of the differences between carrier and land based aviation was weak and never delivered a convincing argument as to what the true effectiveness was between these two basing systems. The only evidence that the report seemed to offer was that the US Air Force provided more sorties than any other air force in the theater. This fact alone may not be enough to prove that land-based air was superior to carrier-based options. Quantity, however, does have a value all its own. Marines and other service members described the Air Force application of airpower in support of CAS during crises in Korea as a "Fire Hose."[286]

The so called "fire hose" system now in use in by the Air Force maybe

---

[284] Ibid.
[285] Ibid.
[286] Larkin, MTACS-2, transcript of oral interview by Captain Nolan J. Beat, 29 June 1951 (USMCHD, CD No.14 of 24).

> effective in theory, but our experience to date has proved conclusively that it is not the answer to close air supporting the Marine meaning of the word. It is readily understood that the big picture should necessarily govern the overall tactical employment of aircraft. However, the efficiency and teamwork of the Marine air-ground system is being tossed overboard under the Air Force system.[287]

The Air Force comparison provided information on the sortie effort and the total assets that each service employed in the Korean theater. It points out that of the total number of sorties flown, the majority were flown by Air Force assets, but it breaks out the Navy and the Marine Corps assets as separate when the original comparison was between land-based and carrier-based air assets. The Marine Corps at this point in the conflict maintained several squadrons on board the escort carriers, the *Badoeng Straits* and the *Sicily*. The Marines also based squadrons in Japan and in South Korea. The land-based Marine units were not broken out in the land-based assets of the report.

The larger total number of aircraft available to the Air Force to conduct CAS was much greater than those available to the Navy or the Marine Corps. A better way to compare the services land-based and sea-based assets were by mission, aircraft type, and relative position of the airfield to the front line. The study looked only at gross figures and it became difficult to determine beyond a simple percentage of sorties what effect land or sea-based assets had on the enemy. Land-based assets seemed to sustain operations for greater periods than did their sea based counterparts. Land-based assets ran an approximate cycle of 15 to 20 days, while Navy sea-based assets went off-station every 10 to 12 days for replenishment.[288]

All the Services contributed to the holding of the Pusan perimeter. Even B-29s flew CAS sorties. Therefore, the Navy's CAS contribution during the Pusan operation was not a unique capability to an aircraft carrier. Had in fact the North Koreans forced the US and UN forces off the Korean peninsula, however the carrier's value would have been clear.

---

[287] Larkin, MTACS-2, transcript of oral interview by Captain Nolan J. Beat, 29 June 1951 (USMCHD, CD No.14 of 24).
[288] Assistant Secretary of the Air Force, June 1972, 5 (ASHAF-A, K143.61).

In August 1950, Admiral Joy asked General MacArthur to make the primary mission for the Navy carriers strikes on "lucrative" enemy targets in North Korea.[289] Task Force 77 became an independent striking force. On 27 August, the carriers steamed northward to strike interdiction targets, demonstrating to flexibility of the carrier. The Air Force was still operating from Japanese bases. The Eighth Army had maintained its defense of the Pusan perimeter. General Walker had nothing but praise for the air support, which the Fifth Air Force had provided to the Eighth Army.

> I am willing to state, said Walker, that no commander had better air support than has been furnished the Eighth Army by the Fifth Air Force. General Partridge and I have worked very closely together since the start of this campaign. We have kept our headquarters together and no request for air support that could possibly be furnished has ever been refused. I will gladly lay my cards right on the table and state that, if it had not been for the air support that we received from the Fifth Air Force we would not have been able to stay in Korea.[290]

The question remains unanswered. Sea-based aviation's value is clearly situational, had we lost Korea in June 1950 the carriers' location relative to the front would have had positive influence on the overall force's target revisit rates, sortie recycle times, sortie generation rates, and the ability to operate from a forward fields although it be afloat. The forward basing of aircraft became the Marines answer to responsiveness and soon after the war began the secret development of a vertical and short take off aircraft, but settling on the British Harrier.[291]

Summary

The characteristics of the Navy-Marine system for CAS in Korea were that it was simple and flexible; communication was swift and direct; aircraft were available and employed on short notice; and the front line unit normally controlled the aircraft dispatched to give it support. Overall, theater command and control of aircraft was centralized at the JOC. The Navy-Marine system centralized command at the TACC/TADC. The control of aircraft employment on CAS missions was decentralized to the maximum extent possible in the Navy-Marine system.

---

[289] Ibid., 8.
[290] Ibid.

The limited availability of artillery early in amphibious operations required the assault force to rely on CAS and naval gunfire to makeup for the lack of adequate field artillery. The Marines normally maintain a regiment of artillery per division or three battalions of three batteries consisting of six guns per battery.[292] The limited objectives and short duration of amphibious operations generally placed greater emphasis on the shock and effectiveness of CAS and naval gunfire. If follow on operations to an amphibious operation were required the Marines would either pass operational control to the Army and return to their Navy assault ships, or be assumed into the Army force.[293]

The Marines deployed to Korea with one under-strength battalion of light 105mm howitzers. The battalion's three batteries consisted of four guns each vice the normal six.[294] The battalion landed in Korea effectively with two combat strength batteries. The shortage of field artillery pieces only compounded Eighth Army's lack of heavy guns.[295] This situation played directly to the Marines strength in relying on CAS to make up for the deficit in artillery and allowed the Marines to excel. At the beginning of the Korean War the entire ground force relied on responsive effective CAS, it was not until 1951 that Eighth Army had determined it had received adequate heavy field artillery to support theater operations.[296]

With the ground forces backed against Pusan and relying heavily on CAS, the Marine entered the war with a sound air-ground control system, a supporting doctrine, and General MacArthur's cooperation to keep the Marine air ground team together. The stage was set for controversy. Tenth Corps' General Almond helped fuel the controversy over CAS provided by the Navy-Marine system versus the Army-Air Force control system. The controversy's dialogue focused on CAS and the two control system

---

[291] Concept of Operations, AV-8 Harrier, Chapters 4, 5, and Summary (McCutcheon personal papers, MCUA PC#464, box 7).
[292] The Korean War Project, "An Evaluation of the Influence of the Marine Corps," Section II-A-16 (MCUA Box 1, folder 27).
[293] Momyer, 60.
[294] The Korean War Project, "An Evaluation of the Influence of the Marine Corps," Section II-A-16 (MCUA Box 1, folder 27).
[295] Millett, "Korea, 1950-1953," 358.
[296] Ibid.

employed in Korea, but the real battle was centered on the single air manager concept found in Army-Air Force doctrine FM 100-20 and FM 31-35. James Winnefeld and Dana Johnson, in their book *Joint Air Operations* sum up this issue well. They said, "Korea was a lesson on the clash of doctrine and combat realities."[297]

The Marines developed sound a doctrine and practiced it in a joint training framework. They coordinated with other services regularly and prepared their air-ground system of control for combat. The Navy-Marine system was based on a short amphibious operation concept that was assigned as a Marine Corps primary mission. The Navy and the Marines had worked through the development of supporting doctrine to reinforce amphibious concepts tested during World War II. They had adopted a communication philosophy dedicated to working combat issues vice administrative issues.[298]

The Army-Air Force communications system, which was geared for a large volume of administrative messages passed over the same communication nets as combat information slowed coordination with the Navy.[299] The Air Force control system weakened by a lack of sound communication equipment early in the war, a limited number of TACPs, and a lack of desire to drop ordnance within 50 to 500 yards of friendly lines struggled through the early war controversies. The JOC restricted system response time and effectiveness by relying on the detailed scripting of the air plan and diverting assets from other missions to provide just in time CAS to ground commanders in contact. The JOC/TACC centralized direction and control over every flight had an impact on the Army-Air Force systems effectiveness. The concept of coordinating authority and the single air asset managers overall control of all theater air assets produced confusion and antagonism between the services.

The Army-Air Force system centralized both command and control at the highest level. Fifth Air Force after January 1951 employed Marine aviation in general support of Eighth Army vice operating in direct support of 1st Marine Division. The Air Force

---

[297] James A. Winnefeld and Dana J. Johnson, *Joint Air Operations: Pursuit of Unity in Command and Control 1942-1991* (Annapolis, Maryland: Naval Institute Press, 1993), 60.
[298] Ibid., 57-58.
[299] Ibid.

increased the volume of CAS sorties, creating a "fire hose" effect with air. Had the Air Force adopted some of the Navy-Marine control system or streamlined the request process, the Air Force could have increased air support effectiveness. The Air Force might have risked adopting a few of the Navy-Marine practices and passed the control of some missions to the TADC or even to assign some missions to a direct support role of ground maneuver units. However, this concept the Air Force saw as a piecemeal approach to applying airpower in war and argued as Air Marshal A. Tedder had against such employment of the Allied airpower during World War II.[300] Strangely, the Air Force did agree that when the tactical situation permitted the JOC would assign Marine air to support Marine ground units.[301] These inter-service arguments over control of airpower demonstrate, as R. J. Overy said in his book *The Air War, 1939-1945,* that cooperation as well as sound strategy were essential components in the use of airpower.[302]

A mutually agreed to joint doctrine in 1950 might have eased the friction between the services somewhat by developing a framework from which to start the development of a coherent joint strategy for Korea. Millett, and Winnefeld and Johnson have stated that the controversy and disagreements between the services continued through the war. Winnefeld points out that the Air Force and the Navy reached some cooperation and understanding only after three years of war.[303] It seems obvious that a mutual doctrine framework would have saved time and energy, but even with an approved joint doctrine disagreements would have arose over its meaning and appropriateness. Cooperation and coordination remained key instruments of employing airpower. Joint doctrine might have provided a common knowledge base for airpower practitioners to reference when at war or going to war, however it did not diminish the requirement for the cooperation necessary to employ force effectively.

The Marines knew immediately that they would need to coordinate with Fifth Air Force in Korea on air issues and acknowledged that FEC assigned Fifth Air Force coordination control over Korea. They disagreed with the Army-Air Force control

---

[300] Momyer, 62.
[301] Ibid.
[302] R.J. Overy, *The Air War 1939-1945*, (New York: Scarborough House, 1980), 76.

system seeing the need to have TACPs to the battalion level and to adapt the control system to decrease the time required to respond to a request for CAS from the ground commander to bombs on target.[304] The Marines worked to coordinate an arrangement with Fifth Air Force to support Marines on the ground with Marines from the air.[305]

As a final analysis of the Korean War the services met in August 1953 to reach an agreement on joint doctrine.[306] The Army, Navy, and Marines expressed the desire to make changes to the Army-Air Force system of control delineated in the joint training directive. They proposed the theater air commander (TAC) allocate air assets in direct support to a ground commander.[307] The services asked for the decentralization of control down to the TADC and fire support coordination center (FSCC) to manage preplanned CAS missions.[308] The conference also produced a recommendation to simplify the request system by streamlining the process to mirror closely the Navy-Marine system where intermediate and senior units and agencies monitor request from line units unless a problem arose.[309] The Air Force rejected these proposals and no agreed joint doctrine was established.[310] Whatever understanding or desire for cooperation and the development of joint doctrine determined by the Korean War experience, it was soon lost on service disagreements.

---

[303] Winnefeld, 50.
[304] Millett, "Korea, 1950-1953," 383.
[305] Ibid., 390.
[306] Ibid., 394.
[307] Ibid.
[308] Ibid.
[309] Ibid.
[310] Ibid., 395.

Chapter 4

CLOSE AIR SUPPORT OPERATIONS AFTER THE KOREAN WAR

The Marine Corps' tactical air arm in Vietnam is a many-splendored force of Marines and diversified aircraft whose sole mission is to support the ground action.

Keith B. McCutcheon, 1971

Introduction

The Korean War ended in 1953. A reasonable person might assume that out of Korea's combined and joint operations a voice would rise up and state with clarity the doctrine all services could support. No epiphany, no prophet, no voice from heaven resonated, just men assigned to joint boards to discuss the issues of doctrine, to recommend proposals, and to defend their service turf.

The Marines and the Air Force were at odds over doctrinal issues that resulted from Korea. The Marines viewed the Air Force view of unity of command under a single air manager as a threat to the Marine air-ground forces. The Air Force discounted the benefits of Marine team training and combined arms action in Korea and then again attempted the same in Vietnam. Oddly, the Marines operated aviation under principles similar to the Air Force single air manager. However, the Air Force saw the Corps as too narrowly focused on tactical issues and not able to see the whole war picture. At the heart of the dispute were differences in command and control and CAS philosophy. These same issues were still present during the Vietnam War. The Marines would resist placing their aviation under the control of Seventh Air Force in Vietnam. However, they would submit and negotiate a deal to maintain some independence to preserve their air-ground team philosophy. In Korea the ground situation dictated air priorities, was the same true in Vietnam?

After Korea, each of the services embarked on reviews of their roles and missions. The services saw the introduction of new ordnance, weapon systems, and communication assets that had direct effect on aviation organizations and tasks. The introduction of these new electronic media technologies in Vietnam influenced the way we fight today. These tools affected CAS doctrine, organization, tactics, techniques, and procedures for all of the services.

Vietnam and CAS Doctrine Refined

There still exists, however, a great variance of opinion as to the employment of tactical air support. This spread of opinion does not exist on the effectiveness of tactical air support, but, rather, upon its control

Lieutenant Colonel Clarence C. DeReus,
Infantry Student,
Command and Generals Staff College,
US Army, 1953

The services embarked on a quest to resolve their differences in accordance with the Joint Action Armed Forces (JAAF) Manual. The services started the process in 1951 and divided joint action among them by functional area. The Air Force acted as executive agent for the Joint Tactical Air Support Board and the Joint Air Transportation Board. The Army established the Joint airborne Troop Board. The Navy chaired the Joint Amphibious Board, while the Marines headed the Joint Landing Board at the Marine Corps Schools. This was an interesting time in doctrinal development. The officers serving as members of these joint boards represented their services but the final decision authority rested with the service chiefs.[311]

The Navy-Marine position on joint amphibious operations seemed to mirror the pre-Korea doctrine of Amphibious Warfare Instructions (USF-6) that all amphibious operations should be task organized and commanded by an admiral and joint task force commander.[312] The Navy would maintain operational control of all forces in the amphibious objective area including the supporting naval force until operational control passed to the landing force commander. The process of phasing control ashore included the control of the functions of aviation.[313] The successful passage of control hinged on the establishment of ship-to-shore communication necessary to coordinate battle action between the landward and seaward

---

[311] Robert Frank Futrell, *Ideas, Concepts, Doctrine: Basic Thinking in the United States Air Force 1907-1960*, vol. 1 (Air University press, Ala. 1989), 401.
[312] Ibid., 404.
[313] Ibid.

sectors.[314] The Air Force fought for a functional component command relationship of a joint staff organization. Air Force leaders argued that the theater air component commander should retain operational control of all air forces even in the amphibious objective area.[315] The Army took the position that amphibious operations represented an enabling force action and that a supreme joint task force commander should maintain operational control over the theater campaign. The Army advocated Army control of air strikes.[316]

The doctrinal debate continued throughout the 1950s. The service arguments had not changed significantly since World War II. Futrell points out that the Air Force advocated centralized control of aviation and lacked confidence in the other services' ability and determination to employ air to its fullest advantage.[317] The Air Force was probably correct in that the Navy, Marines, and the Army might as necessary partition combat aviation into service and unit sectors and control it at the tactical and operational level rather than theater strategic level of command.[318] The Army and the Navy had argued that depending on the situation the decentralization of air to the battlefield commander as the controlling authority may have represented the necessary unity of command for success.[319] Major General Almond, who in Korea desired local control of air forces to increase his combat power and efficiency, could have led the argument.[320] To the Air Force, this narrow local view of the air war would result in a segmentation and subordination of airpower.[321] The Air Force viewed this doctrinal concept as a step backward to pre-World War II aviation. Airpower as a combat force had become too flexible a weapon for local control to employ it effectively.[322]

As the debate over doctrine continued among the services, internal battles raged as well. The Commandant of the Marine Corps in 1955 ordered an aviation broad review of the

---

[314] Ibid.
[315] Ibid.
[316] Ibid., 405.
[317] Ibid., 407.
[318] Ibid.
[319] Ibid.
[320] Department of the Air Force, *An Evaluation of the Effectiveness of the United States Air Force in The Korean Campaign*, Korean Evaluation Project, "Sterns Mission Report," memorandum with attached staff study, from Headquarters Tenth Corps, subj: Army Tactical Air Support Requirements (ASHAF-A, K168.041, vol. 20, tabs 41-42).
[321] Futrell, 404
[322] Ibid., 407.

missions, functions, and tasks of Marine Corps aviation. The Marine Corps aviation review board reviewed and analyzed the mission as:

> The Mission of Marine Corps aviation is to provide air support for the ground components of the Fleet Marine Forces in execution of such missions as may be assigned; and, as a collateral mission, to constitute a replacement for carrier-based air units of the United States Navy.[323]

The board recommended the following tactical functions of Marine aviation: attack, intercept, reconnaissance, transport, control, and service support. The board went further and separated direct air support and counter-air functions as two broadly divided areas of tactical air operations. These two stated types of roles of tactical airpower combined many functions already listed and included, among other tasks, CAS, air defense, interdiction, and the neutralization of enemy air bases and operating areas (offensive counter-air). The board established an organizational structure that enabled the Corps aviation to operate from bases in the U.S. or overseas and from a mix of shore bases and carriers. It also provided for the deployment of parts of the Wing to operate with independent task forces as required.[324]

The board process set the stage for the development of the "M" series Tables of Organization and Equipment which remained the standard of the Corps for the next twenty years.[325] The same process gave rise to a small controversy within higher echelons of the Marine Corps over the direction of Marine aviation and its doctrine.

Lieutenant General MeGee (Chief of Staff to the CMC) wrote a personal letter to the CMC concerning an evaluation and recommendations made by Lieutenant General Merrill B. Twining, the Commanding General, Marine Corps Schools. The CMC originally tasked General Twining with providing with his doctrinal interpretation of air defense functions in amphibious operations. MeGee was concerned that Twining was not confining himself to the task as originally set forth to answer CMC's query, but thought that Twining sought to reopen the question concerning the organization and employment of Marine Corps aviation.[326]

---

[323] Keith B. McCutcheon, "Mission, Functions and Tasks of Marine Corps Aviation", research material Marine Corps Board results review, 1956 (From the Keith B. McCutcheon personal papers PC#464, Box 8, MCUA).
[324] Ibid.
[325] Alan R. Millett, *Semper Fidelis: the History of the United States Marine Corps* (Ontario Canada: The Free Press, 1991), 527.
[326] Vernon E. MeGee, Chief of Staff, Headquarters Marine Corps, letter to Commandant of the Marine Corps, subject: Recommendations of CG Marine Corps Schools, 28 January 1957.

MeGee challenged Twining on his doctrinal interpretations of Marine aviation capability to wage effective war in the air as an independent combat element. MeGee accused Twining of selling Marine air short by limiting it to the role of aerial artillery and airborne motor transport. Twining, he said, would accept as binding on the Marine Corps combat squadrons the entire unrealistic radial limitation of 100 miles, which the Air Force had imposed on the Army's light reconnaissance aircraft.[327]

MeGee questioned the reasoning for accepting the concept of support from anyone other than the Marine Corps' own squadrons who trained especially for amphibious operations. MeGee emphasized that the success or failure of an amphibious operation rested on gaining air supremacy in the zone of operations. He thought that the theater tactical air commander was responsible for the general air defense of the area, while the final defense of the objective area required specially trained squadrons operating under the amphibious commander or the commander of the landing force. MeGee thought that the Air Force would not give the close-in defense of the amphibious objective area the priority it required for successful operations.[328]

Twining voiced concern that the Air Force would challenge the existence of Marine aviation. MeGee did not agree. He did not see the Air Force as interested in Marine aviation because the Marines concerned themselves with the air support mission, a mission he thought the Air Force had no interest in.[329]

The Air Force wanted the control of all air assets in a theater of operations. The Air Force, by pursuing the concept of an air component commander as the single control authority in a theater could accomplish two things. First, as the single controlling authority the Air Force could apply airpower to the full potential of its vision. Second, by pursuing the single control authority concept the Air Force avoided the overhead of maintaining the CAS aircraft of the Marine Corps. The Air Force would have had a difficult time assuming Marine Corps aviation or its programs based on the protection offered the Marine Corps by federal statute.[330]

The Air Force must have had some success in convincing the Marines that Air Force airpower doctrine had some value. MeGee wrote,

Certain Marine planners have been indulging in grandiose and unrealistic flights

---
[327] Ibid.
[328] Ibid.
[329] Ibid.
[330] Ibid.

of fancy with respect to their advocacy of 'wild blue yonder' tactics…he says that there were such misguided souls during WWII and that such thinking was foreign to the concept of integrated air ground operations.[331]

The fact remained for MeGee that the integrated air-ground team of 1957 required Marine air support and the ability to influence the area of operations beyond the amphibious objective area in order to isolate the area and to reduce the enemy's ability to reinforce. Speaking of the proposed one hundred mile limit on Marine tactical aviation MeGee stated, "We hardly need to clip the wings of our combat pilots to keep them from flying outside their assigned orbits."[332] The limitation of aircraft capability based on assigned service missions was a serious miscalculation, violating the principle reason airpower could dominate surface forces, its flexibility.[333] The limitation on Army reconnaissance aircraft range took away a small part of airpower's inherent flexibility.

Air Power Priorities

Doctrinally the air priorities established for each of the services remained similar to what they had been since World War II. The Air Force focused on interdiction and strategic attack. The Marine Corps focused on the principles of CAS. In 1965, the Marines went ashore at Da Nang. The President and the Secretary of Defense supported increased presence of US ground forces and the use of B-52s to support operations in South Vietnam.[334]

This was not the first time that the US had used strategic bombers in a direct support role. Use of the B-52s conjured up memories of Korea when B-29s supported UN forces there. In Korea, the use of strategic bombers was to avert crisis and stop the North Korean and Chinese forces. The situations in Vietnam presented no visible or immediate crisis that would indicate the need for these strategic weapons. The decision to employ B-52s on South Vietnam in a CAS role represented the air equivalent of the grounds final protective fires.[335]

The Johnson administration determined that the place to destroy the North Vietnamese was to attack them in South Vietnam, or "in-country."[336] The focus of the air effort then

---

[331] Ibid.
[332] Ibid.
[333] Futrell, *Ideas, Concepts, Doctrine*, vol. 1, 407.
[334] General William W. Momyer, USAF (ret.), *Air Power in Three Wars (WWII, Korea, Vietnam)* (United States Air Force), 20.
[335] Ibid., 283.
[336] Ibid., 14.

centered on these in-country missions, while advocates of traditional uses of airpower continued to request a shift in priority to increase attacks on the enemy homeland, or "out-of-country" missions.[337] By 1966, the strategy and priority of the air planners placed greater emphasis on attacking strategic and interdiction targets in North Vietnam.[338]

The military seemed no longer able to establish air priorities and to focus the full measure and flexibility of airpower on an adversary due to national strategic concerns. These concerns constrained and restricted airpower's capability to influence the enemy. The on-again-off-again and in-country-out-of-country response and retaliation campaigns seemed to fall short of the concept envisioned by General Curtis LeMay and Admiral U.S. Grant Sharp.[339] Washington seemed to manage and dictate Air Force air priorities, especially for out-of-country missions and to lesser degree for in-country missions. The Air Force doctrinal emphasis had not changed, nor had the other services changed their outlook on air prioritization, Washington chose to constrain airpower and one method of accomplishing this task was through managing the air priorities.

In 1965, Commander-in-Chief, Pacific Command (CinCPac) issued a directive on the conduct and control of air support for Pacific Command and Vietnam.[340] CinCPac stated that the priority mission in Vietnam was CAS. The directive also authorized the supported ground commander to direct CAS aircraft assigned via his local air support agency. A subsequent revision to the original directive issued by CinCPac designated Seventh Air Force as the coordinating authority for all US and allied military air operations in Vietnam.[341] Seventh Air Force was also tasked with establishing an air traffic control system to provide a means to deconflict the air space.[342] The commander of United States Military Assistance Command Vietnam (USMACV) also charged Seventh Air Force with developing joint instructions to ensure integrated and coordinated air operations in SouthVietnam.[343]

---

[337] Ibid., 21.
[338] Ibid., 23.
[339] Ibid.
[340] Keith B. McCutcheon, "Marine Aviation in Vietnam, 1962-1971", *Naval Review* (1971), 135.

[341] Ibid., 136.
[342] Ibid.
[343] Ibid.

The service positions laid out above is but a snapshot of the evolution of air priorities during the Vietnam War. The air priority philosophy of each service had not changed, but the overall influence of Washington on setting the air priorities had increased to the point that these priorities could change hourly if desired. In fact, the communication technology had advanced to the point that the situation room at the White House seemed as informed as the theater commander and began to develop operational air strategies and to change the air priorities.

See diagram, Figure 10, the US & Vietnamese air-ground control system, and Figure 11, the Navy- Marine System used in Vietnam.

Organization of CAS Assets

The National Security Act of 1947 and the Reorganization Act of 1958 divided the services roles, functions, and tasks in terms of air, land, and sea.[344] The Air Force fought to establish the concept of a single air manager in Vietnam. The Air Force felt that two separate systems led to a lack of efficiency. The Air Force believed without centralized control at the highest level that both Seventh Air Force and Marines would both attack the same targets, while other targets would not be attacked.[345] The Marines thought that the Air Force system added layers unnecessarily to request processing and increased response time.[346] The old arguments were still alive and well.

The single air manager became a reality as a result of MACV Directive 95-4 issued 6 May 1965.[347] This MACV directive gave control authority over all Army, Navy, and Air Force aviation assets to Seventh Air Force.[348] MACV excluded the Marines initially on the basis that Marine aviation was organic to the Marine Amphibious Force (MAF). The Marine Tactical Air Control System would exercise control over Marine air.[349] This exclusion prevented Seventh Air Force from centralizing control of all aviation in theater.

ComUSMACV revised its earlier directive in June and designated the Commander Seventh Air Force the Air Force Component Commander to act as the coordinating authority for all air forces in the MACV area. MACV directed CG III MAF to exercise operational control over Marine tactical air forces and to conduct both offensive and defensive operations to include CAS, interdiction, reconnaissance, air superiority, air transport, search and rescue, and other air support as required.[350] The directive additionally instructed III MAF to provide all resources in excess of its organic requirements to Commander Seventh Air Force for his allocation to support other forces and missions.[351]

The Marines at this point relinquished control of air defenses in its sector to the Air Component Commander, Seventh Air Force. Although, the Marines had the means to support

---

[344] Futrell, *Ideas, Concepts, Doctrine*, vol. 2, 277.
[345] Ibid, 283.
[346] Major Michael J. Manuche, "The Single Air Manager in Three Wars: the integration of Marine Air with the Joint Environment", (paper, Quantico, VA: MC C&SC, 1996), 26.
[347] Ibid, 282.
[348] Ibid.
[349] Momyer, 81.
[350] McCutcheon, "Marine Aviation in Vietnam", 136.

their own air defense operations in sector with the dual role F-4 fighter and the radars of the Tactical Air Operations Center (TAOC), it was best in III MAFs view to integrate air defense functions under one authority.[352]

The MAF and the Seventh Air Force signed a Memorandum of Agreement in 1965 that delineated policies, procedures, and responsibilities of each. These policy documents remained in force until 1968 when General Westmoreland stated that it was no longer feasible to limit air assets to a specific area of operation.[353] He desired to employ tactical aviation through the Air Force single air asset manager.[354]

In 1968, the Marines gave up operational control authority of all its air assets to General Momyer, CG, Seventh Air Force. The Marines were directed to make available to the Seventh Air Force for mission direction all its strike, reconnaissance aircraft, and its tactical air control system.[355] Like the term Coordinating Authority used by the Far East Command (FEC) in Korea, Seventh Air Force did not define either operational or mission direction terms used in the directive establishing single management over the Corps' air assets. The term defined in a 1970 follow-on directive issued by Seventh Air Force defined mission or operational direction as,

> The authority delegated to one commander (i.e., Deputy ComUSMACV) to assign specific air task to another commander (i.e., CG, III MAF) on a periodic basis as implementation of a basic mission previously assigned by a superior commander (ComUSMACV).[356]

Senior Marines feared that the change in organizational structure would have increased response times to CAS request. That was not the case. Seventh Air Force modified the command and control system so that it was as responsive for the Marine's original control structure.[357] Fleet Marine Force Pacific (FMFPac) issued a report on operations under the new system.[358] FMFPac measured response time of preplanned missions and found that those time increased from eighteen hours to thirty-eight to fifty hours after the implementation of the

---

[351] Ibid.
[352] Ibid.
[353] Futrell, *Ideas, Concepts, Doctrine*, vol. 2, 282.
[354] Ibid, 283.
[355] McCutcheon, "Marine Aviation in Vietnam", 136.
[356] Ibid, 137.
[357] Ibid.
[358] Manuche, 25.

Seventh Air Force single asset manager under the Air Force air control system.[359] This meant that the planning window available for planners pushed back another day or two. The MTACC schedule writers moved from a one-day planning cycle to a two-day or three-day planning cycle for air. The Marines work around for this was to provide enough preplanned air, based on previous day or weeks schedule to support the scheduled and non-scheduled demands from the line commanders[360].

McCutcheon also points out that the Air Force required 1st MAW to provide daily sortie rates to AFTACC based on a one sortie per day per aircraft. 1st MAW generally exceeded the 1.0 sortie rate, which meant that additional sorties necessary to support tactical air request could launch on order of the Camp Horn Direct Air Support Center (DASC).[361] The DASC was co-located with the III MAF headquarters.[362]

General McCutcheon said of the single management system,

> There is no doubt about whether single management was an overall improvement as far as MACV as a whole was concerned. It was. And there is no denying the fact that, when three Army divisions were assigned to I Corps and interspersed between the two Marine divisions, a higher order of coordination and cooperation was required than previously.[363]

The Air Force viewed the Marine approach to the organization of CAS and CAS employment as a costly way of doing business.[364] The structure of each system was different originally due to the level of command that each service centralized its control organization. General McCutcheon wrote that the two systems worked because of the Marines and the Airmen that ran the systems. The methods used to make the systems work evolved of time by verbal agreements between commanders. McCutcheon stated that no detailed order was written explaining the procedures beyond the initial directive. The Air Force with the Marines improved efficiency by making small changes to the system. General McCutcheon mentioned one such fix was to task a portion of the air support on a weekly basis rather than a daily creating less paper work and creating more time to concentrate on other requested support.

---

[359] Ibid, 26.
[360] McCutcheon, 137.
[361] Ibid.
[362] Ibid.
[363] Ibid.
[364] Momyer, 285.

Means and Effectiveness of Command and Control

The system established for Marine air control in Vietnam grew in size and scope as compared to its Korean forerunner. Still present was the Marine Tactical Air Command Center (MTACC) or Tactical Air Direction Center. In Vietnam, the Marines operated a TADC at Da Nang that was subordinate to the Seventh Air Force Tactical Air Control Center (AFTACC) at Saigon. [365] The two subordinate Marine control agencies were the TAOC and a new organization, the DASC.[366] The TAOC controlled and directed air defense assets and conducted a radar surveillance mission.[367]

The DASC controlled and gave direction to direct air support mission. Its subordinate elements included three Air Support Radar Teams (ASRT) each equipped with a TPQ-10 radar.[368] The ASRT provided the capability to control aircraft in a low visibility environment.[369] The Air Force developed the Sky spot radar system patterned after the TPQ-10.[370] The TPQ-10 could track Marine aircraft equipped with radar beacons for almost fifty miles.[371]

Direct air support efficiency improved in low visibility conditions with the employment of the ASRT radar TPQ-10 and beacon equipped aircraft the A-4, Skyhawk; the A-6, Intruder; and the F-4 Phantom.[372] Knowing the position of the radar and the aircraft supplied enough information for the ASRT radar computer to computed a target solution for the ordnance to be delivered.[373] The ASRT operator transmitted the order to the pilot based on the computer solution.[374] The A-4 was equipped with an autopilot link to the beacon, which enabled the TPQ-10 to control and drop ordnance while the pilot flew hands-off the aircraft controls.[375]

---

[365] McCutcheon, "Marine Aviation in Vietnam," 138.
[366] Ibid.
[367] Ibid.
[368] Ibid,139.
[369] Ibid.
[370] Keith B. McCutcheon, "Air Support for III MEF," *Marine Corps Gazette*, (August 1967), 22.
[371] McCutcheon, "Marine Aviation in Vietnam," 139
[372] Ibid., 139.
[373] Ibid.
[374] Ibid.
[375] Ibid.

The Marines also employed small radar beacons with the TACPs to improve CAS effectiveness.[376] The beacon system known as RABFAC transmitted the FAC's position to the A-6 Intruder radar display.[377] The FAC provided the A-6 with the bearing, range, and the altitude differential between the target and the FAC.[378] The beacon data received by the A-6 was entered into the A-6 weapon system computer improving the A-6 accuracy in bad weather and during night support missions.[379]

The Army and Air Force created additional billets for forward air controllers (FAC) just as the Marines deactivated a number of ground FAC billets during Vietnam.[380] The Corps decided to increase the number of FAC airborne (A) building on the experiences of the Korean War.[381] The Marine Corps integrated FAC(A) and tactical air controllers (TAC)(A) into the control system and removed one ground FAC from each infantry battalion.[382]

The Air Force air-ground system also expanded during Vietnam. Second Air Division (later named, Seventh Air Force) insisted on the doctrinal principles of centralized control. The Air Force established an air support operations center (ASOC) in each military district to help coordinate air operations from the central hub in Saigon, the Air Operations Center (AOC). The AOC became the Combat Operations TACC in an attempt to increase cooperation between the Army and the Air Force.[383] Second Air Division established an in-country TACC and an out-of-country TACC to coordinate strikes in an effort to speed the request process when strikes began in North Vietnam.[384]

The Army had aspirations of operating from a somewhat decentralized control structure with organic helicopter assets. The Army established a separate Tactical Air Support Element (TASE) initially, but within months co-located with the AOC to process tactical air request and to ensure proper coordination.[385] The new air-ground coordination system of the Army an the

---

[376] Ibid., 141.
[377] Ibid.
[378] Ibid.
[379] Ibid.
[380] Futrell, *Ideas, Concepts, Doctrine*, vol. 2, 300.
[381] McCutcheon, "Marine Aviation in Vietnam," 140-141.
[382] Ibid.
[383] Futrell, *Ideas, Concepts, Doctrine*, vol. 2, 299.
[384] Ibid., 300
[385] Ibid.

Air Force adjusted the classic air command and control system principled on centralized control and decentralize operations.[386]

The ASOCs became DASCs. The Air Force DASCs subordinate to the TACC functioned as fast reaction control centers designed to process immediate requests for air support quickly with pre-assigned air assets.[387] The TACC Tactical air request arrived at the DASC from the TACPs over an Air Force request net monitored by higher headquarters. Silence was consent; otherwise, the higher authority would disapprove the request.[388] This system began to look similar to the classic Marine air control system.

The Air Force under this system coordinated air requests on a day-to-day basis by proportioning assets to air tasks.[389] By April 1965, the Air Force air component commander, provided CAS to ground units in South Vietnam.[390] CAS was the highest priority mission based on guidance from General Westmoreland and Secretary McNamera's who emphasized the war in South Vietnam.[391] According to General Momyer the ground commander controlled the air support planning and request processes. He developed the attack plan and target priorities in coordination with his other fire support assets.[392] Aerial weapons applied in close air support operations for the Army became the Army's weapon of choice as the coordination process improved.[393] Seventh Air Force could not measure the effectiveness of the CAS program and began to challenge the return on the heavy investment in CAS missions.[394] The Army and the South Vietnamese became very dependent on the fire hose of firepower provided by CAS.[395] Futrell cites a 1966 Office of Secretary of Defense (OSD) study that questioned the effectiveness of CAS and determined that 65% of the total tonnage dropped may or may not have targeted the enemy.[396] Futrell also quoted General Quesada who concluded the

---
[386] Ibid., 299.
[387] Ibid., 300.
[388] Ibid.
[389] Ibid.
[390] Ibid., 301.
[391] Ibid.
[392] Ibid., 301-302.
[393] Ibid., 300.
[394] Ibid., 302.
[395] Ibid.
[396] Ibid.

expenditure of tactical air power over South Vietnam focused largely on bombing forest and was a product of Army thinking.[397]

{One explanation for the Air Force's disenchantment with this program was the failure to obtain solid BDA on targets attacked. Guesses just were not good enough in limited war. The applied pressure measured to gain submission or compliance with demands was just too difficult a mark to hit for the type of warfare executed in Vietnam. A similar anomaly may have occurred in Bosnia and Kosovo in the late 1990s.}

Momyer argued, the Vietnam War brought the single air manager a step closer to accepted practice. McCutcheon stated that the single air manager was an improvement and that given the complexity of the task organization in I Corps, it was required. Both the Air Force and the Marine leadership had to reach agreement on the issues and procedures necessary to implement this program. Korea and Vietnam proved that CAS involves a high order of cooperation and coordination starting with the senior leadership.

III MAF did not receive all of its air support from organic resources within the single management system. Neither was it the exclusive user of its own assets. The Marines, the Navy, the Air Force, the South Vietnamese Air Force, and even the Royal Australian Air Force (RAAF) provided air support to US and Vietnamese ground forces. However, III MAF did have first claim to its own assets, so most of the time Marines supported Marines.[398]

Basing in Vietnam

When the Vietnam War began for the Americans, there were only three major airfields in South Vietnam.[399] All needed repairs. Da Nang in I Corps required a 10,000 ft. runway and expansion of facilities. Bien Hoa and Tan Son Nhut each would require replacement runways shortly after combat aircraft started using them.[400] The Air Force planned to up build additional airstrips at Cam Ranh Bay, Phan Rang, Phu Cat, Tuy Hoa, and Chu Lai with the

---

[397] Ibid., 303.
[398] General Keith B. McCutcheon, USMC, interviewed by Oral History Unit, Major Thomas E. Donnelly, USMC, Historical Division Headquarters U.S. Marine Corps, 22 April 1971.
[399] McCutcheon, 128.
[400] Momyer, 271.

decision to deploy Marine and Army units to South Vietnam.[401] Additional bases in South Vietnam provided opportunity to disperse and open access to the additional Marine and Army air units entering South Vietnam.[402] The Marines took action to build a short airfield at Chu Lai based on discussions between Genral Westmoreland and Admiral Sharp.[403]

It was through Lieutenant General Victor Krulak's foresight that a short airfield was built for tactical support at Chu Lai.[404] The Marines developed the concept of operating a carrier type operation from short landing and take-off fields in the mid 1950s.[405] They prefabricated an instant airfield that could be handled and set up by a Marine Air Group of two to three squadrons.[406] The facilities included runway surface, arresting gear, hardstand, and taxiway. The field also included air control facilities, refueling, rearming points, maintenance bays, and other logistical and billeting requirements. The time allotted for setup was 72 to 96 hours.[407] The runway surface consisted of aluminum interconnecting planks, called Am-2 matting.[408] These moveable expeditionary runways provide insight into the Marines interest in gaining access to unimproved areas that might not have the necessary air facilities to support jets or even extended helicopter operations.

The Marines have long been interested in the early phasing ashore of Marine aviation units and the stationing of air support assets close to the battle area. These efforts center on the axiom to provide to the best air support possible for ground forces. Arming and refueling points established well forward improve recycle and response time where limited or no

---

[401] Ibid.
[402] Ibid.
[403] McCutcheon, "Marine Aviation in Vietnam," 128.
[404] Ibid.
[405] Ibid, 129.
[406] Ibid.
[407] Ibid, 128.

traditional airbases exist. Airfields suitable for conventional operations in locations adjacent to the area of operations may not be available or obtainable for diplomatic reasons.

Basing provides access or the potential for access to an area. Carrier and expeditionary airfields provide a solution when denied access or facilities are not adequate or available. The Air Force has focused on extending range and aerial refueling. These systems provide access but are limited by recycle times, available airframes, and limited time in the objective area. A B-2 bomber's capability to fly a thirty-hour mission is very impressive. But the sustainment of these missions operating over extended periods in a mid-size conflict would force us to forward deploy even these long-range lethal weapons. The flexibility offered our nation by having both land-based long-range aircraft and carrier-based and expeditionary air assets adds exponentially to national security.

---

[408] McCutcheon, interviewed by Oral History Unit

Chapter 5

CONCLUSION

The tactical air control system was surely one of the unquestioned successes for our airpower in Vietnam.

General William W. Momyer, Commanding General, Seventh Air Force

During World War II, two doctrinal air-ground systems emerged, an Army-Air Force system and a Navy-Marine system. However, inter-service coordination and cooperation became a problem. Lieutenant Colonel Keith McCutcheon proposed a solution during the Philippines Campaign based on necessity to employ air in a joint operation. The key to proficiency and control of CAS in the Philippines Campaign was communication, organization, training, coordination, and integration. Doctrinal debates, service bureaucracy, personal politics, and deal making overshadowed the potential solution.

The Korean War did not resolve the problems of controlling tactical aircraft in combat. The two systems of control still existed. The doctrinal debate, not settled before the start of the war, led the Marines to attempt to strike a deal with General MacArthur. The two systems of air control employed during the early months of the Korean War brought about a controversy between the Army and the Air Force over the effectiveness of Air Force CAS compared with CAS provided by the Marines. The Air Force, after an in-depth study and comparison of the air-ground systems used at the beginning of the Korean War, decided that the Air Force air-ground system and doctrine was sound. Under the direction and leadership of General Stratemeyer, the FEAF continued to employ the Army-Air Force system and successfully brought Marine aviation under the control of a single air asset manager. Although CAS for UN ground forces seemed to improve under the Army-Air Force air-ground system, the level of success never reached the acclaim the Marines had achieved during the first six months of the war.

The doctrinal issues of World War II and Korea continued into the Vietnam War. The doctrinal conflict over the two systems of air-ground control centered on old disputes over air support philosophy, the efficiency and effectiveness of CAS, and the command and control structure and process. Vietnam most certainly was a turning point in the effective integration of the two air-ground control systems operated by under Army-Air Force and Navy-Marine service doctrine.

In the Vietnam War, General Momyer thought the single air manager was brought a step closer to accepted practice. McCutcheon wrote that in Vietnam the single air manager was an improvement, and that given the complexity of the task organization in I Corps it was required. Both Air Force and Marine leadership having reached an agreement on the issues and procedures, implemented a program focused on cooperation and coordination. The impression that emerged from Korea and Vietnam regarding successful employment of CAS is that it involves a high order of cooperation and coordination starting with the senior leadership.

The Air Force believed in a single asset manager over the years and that had caused some problems in command relations between it and the Marines, especially at the end of the Korean War. A controversy arose from the Vinson investigation, due to reports, both official and unofficial, that troops in the field had received less than adequate support from the Air Force. This fueled the controversy but also called attention to the lack of joint integration and cooperation in Korea.

The debate over control of assets and the single asset manager for air is still with us. The Marines have agreed to the single management concept in the form of the JFACC. They have established scenarios that create a role for the Marines to fill the JFACC position in expeditionary operations to prepare for follow-on air forces.

The appointment of a single authority focused on the direction of the air effort is attributed to the airpower accomplishments of the Gulf War. Before the Gulf War nearly all officers in the Air Force would refer to the JFACC as a commander. Marine officers might question the term commander and call the JFACC a coordinator. During the Gulf War, each service was organized into control sectors responsible for its own piece of the battle-space. This was a workable relationship, although it did not seem to fit the single manager doctrinal approach to the problem.

The same issues raised during World War II, Korea, and Vietnam are still basic talking points for the services today. The CAS issue for the Air Force surrounds the efficiency of airpower in relation to the overall war, while the Army and Marines focus on CAS as a necessary tool of combat power which adds to the ground commander's efficiency in relation to the overall war.

The most important thing in any of the cases studied was not which system was used for close support but that the system had to satisfy three minimum requirements for adequate CAS: 1) The system must permit the battalion commander to request emergency air support directly from the control center; 2) it must provide for the availability of aircraft over the target area within minutes; and 3) it must provide a competent air controller in a forward observation post where he can see friendly front lines, the aircraft, and the target to direct a strike to occur generally at a range of 50 to 500 yards from friendly lines.[409]

The key to achieving the three minimum requirements for CAS are found where I began this study. Lieutenant Colonel McCutcheon in the Philippines Campaign used cooperation, coordination, and training to integrate the air and ground forces. In Vietnam, McCutcheon worked with Seventh Air Force and through cooperation and coordination, US CAS succeeded.

Tactical air forces provided ground units with a weapon that was multi-mission capable. Tactical aircraft in Vietnam began to blur the lines between tactical and strategic aircraft. Aviation fires were immediately available to ground units upon request. The same airframe could conduct an interdiction or strategic attack in the same day. Tactical air should not be limited to fighting beyond the range of ground fires, nor should tactical aviation be limited to fighting short of the FSCL. Airpower was and is a weapon of great flexibility. Aircraft, unlike artillery, is not limited by firing position. Aircraft can provide artillery-like effects and at the same time the aircraft is much more.

The secret to success in CAS operations is teamwork, coordination, and determination to make the system work. The level of commitment at the highest level of command, down the chain, weighs heavily on success or failure. In World War II, Korea,

---

[409] Major General V. E. McGee, "Tactical Air Support for Ground Forces," *Marine Corps Gazette* (December 1955), 17.

and Vietnam, leaders came to a reasonable course of action and a workable solution. Major General Vernon MeGee, a Marine CAS advocate wrote.

> All the functions of aviation are critical to success and air support sometimes must be temporarily excluded as a priority mission.... In conclusion, I would like to say for the record that as an airman I am fully cognizant of the necessity for our having and independent strategical air force; that I realize the paramount requirement of adequate air defense; but that the raison d'etre of Marine Corps Aviation per se, is the capability to closely support the ground elements of the Fleet Marine Forces.[410]

---

[410] Ibid, 15.

Bibliography

Air Force Bulletin No. 1 (AFB 1). Department of the Air Force, Washington, D.C., 21 May1948. In Korean Evaluation Project, "Report on Air Operations" Barcus Mission Report. Supporting Letters. Maxwell AFB, AL: AFHRA file K168.041, vol. 20.

Almond, Major General Edward M. To Commanding General, FEAF and to Commander, USNF-FE. Joint letter. Subject: Coordination of Air Effort of Far East Air Forces and United States Naval Forces, Far East, 8 July 1950. Maxwell AFB, AL: AFHRA file K168.041-1.

———, GHQFEC, Chief of Staff, by command of General MacArthur, to Commander, United States Naval Forces Far East (NAVFE), and Commanding General, Far East Air Forces. Letter. Subject: Coordination of the Air Effort of Far East air Forces and United States Naval Forces Far East, AG370.2, 8 July 1950. Maxwell AFB, AL: AFHRA file K168.041-2.

Antone, First Lieutenant A.D., VMF-311, 1st Marine Aircraft Wing, FMF. Interviewed by 1st Marine Historical Platoon, 23 January 1951. In CD-ROM collection of Korean War Historical Documents, USMCHD CD No.14 of 24.

Assistant Secretary of the Air Force. "A Quantitative Comparison between Land-based and Carrier-based Air During the Korean War." June 1972. Maxwell AFB, AL: AFHRA file K 143.61.

Bagnall, Major E.E. et al., *FAC [Forward Air Controller] Course book.* Headquarters, Marine Air Control Group 2, 1st Marine Aircraft Wing, Fleet Marine Force. 26 August 1952. Quantico, VA: MCUA, Keith B. McCutcheon Personal Collection (PC) #464, Box 3.

Cunningham, Major Alfred A. "Value of Aviation to the Marine Corps," *Marine Corps Gazette*, September 1920, 225-26.

Boldman, Captain James D. Transcript of oral interview by S.W. Higginbotham, 1st Provisional Historical Platoon, 24 January 1951. Washington D.C.: USMCHD, CD-ROM collection of Korean War Historical Documents, CD No.14 of 24.

Cates, C.B., Commandant of the Marine Corps (CMC). Memorandum. To Chief of Naval Operations (CNO). Subject: Employment of 1st MAW in Support of 1st Marine Division in Korea, 31 May 1951. Quantico, VA: MCUA "Korean War Project." Box 14, folder 15.

Clark, General Mark, Chief of US Army Field Forces. Memorandum. To Chief of Staff of the Army. Subject: Tactical Air Support for Ground Forces, 13 September 1951. Carlisle, PA: http://carlisle-www.army.mil/cgi-bin/usamhi/DL/

Conant, Captain Rodger, VMF-311. Transcript of oral interview by J.I. Kiernan, 23 January 1951. Washington D.C.: USMCHD, CD-ROM collection of Korean War Historical Documents, CD No.14 of 24.

Concept of Operations, AV-6 Harrier. Quantico, VA: MCUA, Keith B. McCutcheon Personal Collection (PC) #464, Box 7.

Craig, Major General Edward A. Transcript of oral interview by 1st Historical Platoon, Headquarters, U.S. Marine Corps "The Pusan Perimeter through Pohang

Commitment," 8 May 1951. Washington D.C.: USMCHD, CD-ROM collection of Korean War Historical Documents, CD No.14 of 24.

Cram Jack R., and Col Charles L. Banks, "Win, Place, and Show for the Jets," *Marine Corps Gazette* December 1951, 15-17.

Crowe, Major William E., Operations Officer, VMF-311. Transcript of oral interview by S.W. Higginbotham, 22 January 1951. Washington D.C.: USMCHD, CD-ROM collection of Korean War Historical Documents, CD No.14 of 24.

Department of the Air Force, *An Evaluation of the Effectiveness of the United States Air Force in The Korean Campaign*, Barcus Report and Streans Report. Maxwell AFB, AL: AFHRA K168.04-1, vols. 1 through 29, December 1950.

Eisenhower, Dwight D., Chief of Staff of the Army. Memorandum. To Secretary of Defense. Subject: Tactical Air Support, Stearns Mission, 3 November 1947. Maxwell AFB, AL: AFHRA file ASHAF-A K168.041-1, vol. 20.

———. Letter. To W. Stuart Symington, The Secretary of the Air Force. Subject: Secret memorandum on Tactical Air Support, signed 3 November 1947, March 8, 1950. Maxwell AFB, AL: AFHRA file K168.041-1, vol. 20.

Finletter, Mr., Mr. McCone, General Twining, General McIntyre, General Smith, Professor Leach. Memorandum for the Record. Subject: Summary of Conclusions Reached at meeting 10 January 1951. Maxwell AFB, AL: AFHRA file K168.041-1, vol. 20.

Fliesher, Wade F., Colonel, USAF, Deputy Chief of Legislative Division. Memorandum. To General Hall. Subject: Excerpts from Marine Corps Testimony on Tactical Aviation given to the House Armed Services Committee, 4 and 5 October 1950. Maxwell AFB, AL: AFHRA file K168.041-1, vol. 20.

Futrell, Robert Frank *Ideas, Concepts, and Doctrine: Basic Thinking in the United States Air Force 1907-1960*, vol. 1. Maxwell AFB, AL: Air University Press, 1989.

———. *Ideas, Concepts, Doctrine: Basic Thinking in the United States Air Force 1961-1984*, vol. 2. Maxwell, AFB, AL: Air University Press, 1989.

———. *The United States Air Force in Korea 1950-1953*. Air Force History and Museums Program, 2000.

General Headquarters Southwest Pacific Area. Standing Operating Procedure (SOP) for CLOSE AIR SUPPORT, no. 6, Close Air Support, 24 June 1943. Quantico, VA: MCUA, Keith B. McCutcheon Personal Collection (PC) #464, Box 3.

———, Standing Operation Procedure instruction, no.16/2, Close Air Support, 26 September1944. Quantico, VA: MCUA, PC #464, Box 3.

Gottschalk, Major Vincent J., Commander, VMO-6, 1st MAW. Transcript of oral interviewed by Captain S.W. Higginbotham, 31 March 1951. Washington D.C.: USMCHD, CD-ROM collection of Korean War Historical Documents, CD No.14 of 24.

Headquarters Marine Corps. "An Evaluation of Air Operations Affecting the U.S. Marine Corps in World War II." Washington, D.C.: HQMC 1945. Quantico, VA: MCUA, PC #464, Box 4.

Huston, Dr. James A. "The Tactical Use of Air Power during World War II: The Army Experience," *Military Review* July 1952, 32-48.

Isely, Jeter A., and Philip A. Crowl. *The Marines and Amphibious War: Its Theory, and Its Practice in the Pacific* Princeton, N.J.: Princeton University Press, 1951.

Jacobs, W. A. "The Battle for France, 1944." In *Case Studies in the Development of Close Air Support*. Edited by Benjamin Franklin Cooling. Washington, DC: OAFH, 1990.

Johnson, Wray. "Biplanes and Bandits: The Early U.S. Airpower Experience in Small Wars." Draft Paper, School of Advanced Airpower Studies (SAAS), 2001.

Larkin, Major Wade W., Commanding Officer, Marine Tactical Air Control Squadron (MTACS) 2. Transcript of oral interview by Captain Nolan J. Beat, 29 June 1951. Washington D.C.: USMCHD, CD-ROM collection of Korean War Historical Documents, CD No.14 of 24.

Leach, W. Burton, Department of the Air Force, Office of the Secretary. Open Memorandum. Subject: Status of "Korean Evaluation Project," 9 January 1951. Maxwell AFB, AL: AFHRA file K168.041-1, v-20.

Lewis, Michael. "Lieutenant General, Ned Almond, USA: A Ground Commanders Conflicting view with Airmen over CAS Doctrine and Employment." SAAS thesis, Air University, June 1996.

Magin, Captain William, VMF-311. Transcript of oral interview by S.W. Higginbotham, 23 January 1951. Washington D.C.: USMCHD, CD-ROM collection of Korean War Historical Documents, CD No.14 of 24.

Manuche, Major Michael J. "The Single Air Manager in Three Wars: the integration of Marine Air with the Joint Environment." Paper, Quantico, VA: MC C&SC, 1996.

Marine Corps Board Study. *Evaluation of the Influence of the Marine Corps Forces on the Course of the Korean War*. 4 August 1950-15 December 1951, vol. 1. Quantico, VA: MCUA "Korean War Project." Box 1, folder 27.

McAloney, Holt. "Is Air Support Effective." *The Marine Corps Gazette*. November 1945, 38-41.

McCutcheon, Major General Keith B. "Air Support for III MEF." *Marine Corps Gazette*. August 1967, 18-23.

———. "Air Support Techniques." *Marine Corps Gazette*. April 1946, 23-24. Quantico, VA: MCUA, PC#464, box 3.

———, USMC, Group Operations Officer, Marine Aircraft Group-24, First Marine Aircraft Wing. "Close Air Support Aviation." Staff Notes, Draft Report on Training Problems Post Philippines Campaign October 1944, 119-136. Quantico, VA: MCUA, PC#464, box 3.

———. "Close Air Support SOP." *Marine Corps Gazette*. August 1945, 48-50.

———. "Guided Missiles." Lecture. Marine Corps Volunteer Reserve Unit in Philadelphia, Pa., 9 February 1949. Quantico, VA: MCUA, PC#464, Box 5.

———, "Marine Air Control Group." Draft article dated 4 Sep 46. Quantico, VA: MCUA, PC #464, Box 4

———. "Marine Aviation in Vietnam, 1962-1971." *Naval Review*. 1971, 123-155.

———. Transcript of interviewed by Oral History Unit. Conducted by Major Thomas E. Donnelly, USMC, Historical Division Headquarters U.S. Marine Corps. 22 April 1971. Quantico, VA: MCUA, PC#464, Box 12.

———. "Mission, Functions and Tasks of Marine Corps Aviation." Research material Marine Corps Board results review, 1956. Quantico, VA: MCUA, PC#464, Box 8.

———. "Marine Corps Assault Aircraft Transports." Presentation at the SAE Golden Anniversary Aeronautic Meeting, Hotel Statler, New York, NY, April 18-21, 1955. Quantico, VA: MCUA, PC #464, Box 4.

MeGee, MajGen V. E. "Tactical Air Support for Ground Forces." *Marine Corps Gazette.* December 1955, 12-17.

———, Chief of Staff, Headquarters Marine Corps. Letter. To Commandant of the Marine Corps. Subject: Recommendations of CG Marine Corps Schools, 28 January 1957.

Meuller, Major Elton, Operations Officer, Marine Tactical Air Control Squadron (MTACS) 2. Transcript of oral interview by Captain Nolan J. Beat, 13 December 1950. Washington D.C.: USMCHD, CD-ROM collection of Korean War Historical Documents, CD No.14 of 24.

Millett, Allan R. "Korea, 1950-1953." In *Case Studies in the Development of Close Air Support.* Edited by Benjamin Franklin Cooling. Washington, D.C.: OAFH USAF, 1990.

———. *Semper Fidelis: the History of the United States Marine Corps.* Ontario Canada: The Free Press, 1991.

Miser, Hugh J. *Operations Analysis Report no. 10: Aircraft Service Performance Evaluation Maintenance Workloads Generated in Korean Combat.* Washington, D.C.: Operations Analysis Division, Director of Operations, Deputy Chief of Staff, Operations, Headquarters United States Air Force. Maxwell AFB, AL: AFHRA file K143.042-41.

Momyer, William W. *Airpower in Three Wars (WWII, Korea, Vietnam).* Washington, D.C., Department of the United States Air Force, no date listed.

Overy, R.J. *The Air War 1939-1945.* New York, NY: Scarborough House, 1980.

Pixton, Lieutenant Colonel Allan G. "Close Air Support in Amphibious Operations," *Military Review.* August 1953, 27-34.

Sbrega, John "Southeast Asia." In *Case Studies in the Development of Close Air Support.* Edited by Benjamin Franklin Cooling. Washington, DC: OAFH, 1990.

Smith, Kevin L. "General Keith B. McCutcheon, USMC: A Career Overview-From the Dauntless to Da Nang." Masters Thesis, Marine Command and Staff, 1999.

Stratemeyer, Lieutenant General G.E., Commanding General, FEAF. Memorandum. To Douglas MacArthur, General of the Army. Subject: Naval Units, 8 July 1950. Maxwell AFB, AL: AFHRA file K168.041-1, v-9.

———. Commanding General, FEAF. Letter. To General of the Army, Douglas MacArthur. Subject: Close Support for Ground Troops in Korea, 17 July 1950. Maxwell AFB, AL: AFHRA file K168.041-1.

Syrett, David "The Tunisian Campaign, 1942-43." In *Case Studies in the Development of Close Air Support.* Edited by Benjamin Franklin Cooling. Washington, DC: OAFH, 1990.

Taylor, Joe Gray "American Experience in the Southwest Pacific." In *Case Studies in the Development of Close Air Support.* Edited by Benjamin Franklin Cooling. Washington, DC: OAFH, 1990.

Teller, Captain "Guided Missiles for Naval Operational Employment." Naval War College Paper, n.d. Quantico, VA: MCUA, PC#464, Box 5.

The Korean War Project, "The Marine Corps Board Study: An Evaluation of the Influence of the Marine Corps Forces on the Course of the Korean War." Quantico, VA: MCUA, Box 1, folders 27and 28.

Timberlake, General Edwin J., Vice Commander, 5th Air Force. Transcript of USAF Evaluation Group Recorded Interview by Colonel J.B. Tipton, Operations, FEAF. Maxwell AFB, AL: AFHRA file K168.041-2.

US House. *"Lessons of the Air War in Korea."* Extension of Remarks of the Honorable Melvin Price of Illinois in the House of Representatives. 81st Congress, 2d Session. *Appendix to the Congressional Record.* 96, part 18, (Thursday, December 7, 1950): A7541.

US House. *Vinson Special Subcommittee: Hearings extract, H. Res. 617, On Manpower, Committee on Armed Services.* Tuesday, October 3, 1950. Maxwell AFB, AL: AFHRA file K168.041-1, vol. 20.

Vinson, Carl Chairman, House, Committee on Armed Services. Letter. To General Hoyt S. Vandenberg, USAF Chief of Staff. Subject: Invitation to attend special subcommittee meetings, 2 August 1950. Maxwell AFB, AL: AFHRA file K168.041-1, vol. 20.

Walsh, James T., Colonel, Adjutant General, General Headquarters XIV Corps, for Major General Griswald, Commanding. Memorandum. Number 23. Subject: SOP for Close Air Support, 10 Oct 1944. Quantico, VA: MCUA PC#464, Box 3.

Winnefeld James A., and Dana J. Johnson. *Joint Air Operations: Pursuit of Unity in Command and Control 1942-1991.* Annapolis, Maryland: Naval Institute Press, 1993.

Wykeham-Barnes, P.G. "Air Power Difficulties in the Korean." *Journal of the Royal United Service Institution.* Great Britain, May 1952. Reproduced in *Military Review*. April 1953, 73-81.

Printed in Great Britain
by Amazon.co.uk, Ltd.,
Marston Gate.